Taking Your iPhoto '11 to the Max

Michael Grothaus

Apress®

Taking Your iPhoto '11 to the Max

ISBN-13 (pbk): 978-1-4302-3551-4

ISBN-13 (electronic): 978-1-4302-3552-1

Printed and bound in the United States of America (POD)

President and Publisher: Paul Manning
Lead Editor: Steve Anglin
Development Editor: Douglas Pundick
Technical Reviewer: Steve Sande
Editorial Board: Steve Anglin, Mark Beckner, Ewan Buckingham, Gary Cornell, Jonathan Gennick, Jonathan Hassell, Michelle Lowman, Matthew Moodie, Jeff Olson, Jeffrey Pepper, Frank Pohlmann, Douglas Pundick, Ben Renow-Clarke, Dominic Shakeshaft, Matt Wade, Tom Welsh
Coordinating Editor: Kelly Moritz
Copy Editor: Kim Wimpsett
Compositor: MacPS, LLC
Indexer: BIM Indexing & Proofreading Services
Artist: April Milne
Cover Designer: Anna Ishchenko

Photo Credit: Michael Grothaus

Distributed to the book trade worldwide by Springer Science+Business Media, LLC., 233 Spring Street, 6th Floor, New York, NY 10013. Phone 1-800-SPRINGER, fax (201) 348-4505, e-mail orders-ny@springer-sbm.com, or visit www.springeronline.com.

For information on translations, please e-mail rights@apress.com, or visit www.apress.com.

Apress and friends of ED books may be purchased in bulk for academic, corporate, or promotional use. eBook versions and licenses are also available for most titles. For more information, reference our Special Bulk Sales–eBook Licensing web page at www.apress.com/info/bulksales.

To my mother, Rose "Pookie" Grothaus, who takes way too long when looking at photos.

—Michael

Contents at a Glance

Contents

About the Author

 **Michael Grothaus** is an American novelist and journalist living in London. He was first introduced to Apple computers in film school and went on to use them for years to create award-winning films. However, after discovering many of Hollywood's dirty little secrets while working for 20th Century Fox, he left and spent five years with Apple as a consultant. He's since moved to London and earned his master's degree in creative writing. His first novel, *Epiphany Jones*, is a story about trafficking and America's addiction to celebrity.

Currently, Michael is a staff writer at AOL's popular tech news site The Unofficial Apple Weblog (TUAW.com), where he writes about all things Mac. He's also a contributing writer to the online men's lifestyle magazine, Asylum.com. Additionally, Michael has written several other books for Apress, including *Taking Your iPad to the Max* and *Taking Your iPod touch to the Max, 2nd edition*. When not writing, Michael spends his time traveling Europe, Northern Africa, and Asia. You can reach him at www.michaelgrothaus.com and www.twitter.com/michaelgrothaus.

About the Technical Reviewer

 **Steve Sande** has been a loyal fan of Apple technology since buying his first Mac in 1984. Originally trained as a civil engineer, Steve's career as an IT professional blossomed in the 1990s. A longtime blogger, Steve is an editor at The Unofficial Apple Weblog (TUAW.com), the author of Taking Your iPad to the Max, Taking Your iPhone 4 to the Max, and three books about Apple's iWeb application, and a collaborator on the recent Apress title *Taking Your iPad to the Max*. Steve is certified as an Apple Certified Technical Consultant and is the founder and owner of Raven Solutions, LLC, a company specializing in support and system consulting for Apple devices. He lives with his wife of 31 years and an aging (but feisty) cat in Highlands Ranch, Colorado.

Acknowledgments

Thanks to Steve Sande, my tech reviewer on this book and my coauthor on several other books. Also thanks to Kelly, Kim, Douglas, and the rest of the incredible team at Apress. And let's not forget the entire gang at TUAW.com and also all my friends and family who appear in the photos in this book. Finally, thanks to Jerry Dresden and Hannah Kurylenko: you two have shown me parts of the world—and humanity—both frightening and beautiful, which most people will never even know exists.

Introduction

If you have this book in your hands, you're a person who enjoys photography and wants to get more out of your photographs. You're also probably at least somewhat familiar with Apple's iPhoto application; maybe you've played around with it, but getting to know everything it can do seems daunting. Not to worry, this book is for you.

When I worked for Apple, I learned that the number-one reason people switched to a Mac is so they can use the incredible iLife suite of software, which iPhoto is part of, to manage their digital lives. Matter of fact, iPhoto was so popular and enticing that Apple's sales staff were instructed to lure "switchers" (Windows users who were thinking of buying a Mac) by demoing iPhoto to them before showing them anything else on the Mac. The reason for this is obvious: the number-one digital device everyone owns is a camera, and we record our lives in photographs more than in any other medium. And now the number-one photography application for photography hobbyists is iPhoto '11.

You've got the Mac, you've got the camera, and you've got the digital photos—now get this book. It ties everything together for you and helps you make organizing, navigating, sharing, and editing your photos more fun than you ever thought possible. Don't be intimidated by photo editing either. There's no right way or wrong way to do it. And there's no hard-and-fast rules what a "good" photograph should be like. Matter of fact, the only "should" for photographers is that they should have an understanding of the tools available to them—and iPhoto '11 gives you those tools in a tidy little package.

Taking Your iPhoto '11 to the Max is the book you've been looking for to help you take your photographs to the next level. Now, turn to Chapter 1, and let's get started!

Michael Grothaus

Getting Familiar with iPhoto '11

Before you can begin using any program on your computer, it's important to familiarize yourself with the program's interface. And before you begin familiarizing yourself with the program's interface, it's important that you have all the necessary prerequisites to run the program in the first place.

In this chapter, you'll learn about all the requirements you need to run iPhoto and use it to its fullest. You'll also take a look at the iPhoto interface so you can easily return to this chapter to reference what is where in iPhoto '11.

Getting iPhoto '11

iPhoto '11 is part of Apple's iLife '11 digital lifestyle suite. The entire suite consists of iMovie, iDVD, GarageBand, and iWeb in addition to iPhoto. There are three ways to get iPhoto '11 and the latest iLife suite:

- **Buy a Mac:** iLife '11 ships on every Apple computer bought after November 2010. If you bought your Mac after that time, it will have the latest iLife software, including iPhoto '11.

- **Buy iLife '11 on a DVD:** This option is for those of you who bought Macs before November 2010. If you're in this group, you'll have iLife '09 or earlier on your Mac. You can buy the latest iLife '11 suite from an Apple Store for $49. Inside the box will be a DVD containing the full version of all the iLife apps. Apple doesn't offer iLife upgrades for a reduced price.

■ **Buy iPhoto '11 from the Mac App Store:** This is a great option for those of you who already own a Mac but don't have the latest iLife suite—and wouldn't necessarily use all the applications if you did. The Mac App Store launched in January 2011 and offers Mac users an easy way to purchase and install Mac apps. You can launch the Mac App Store from your Dock or Applications folder on any Mac running OS X 10.6.6 or newer. iPhoto '11 costs $14.99, which is a significant savings over the entire iLife '11 suite.

iPhoto '11 System Requirements

The first thing you need in order to use iPhoto '11 is an Apple computer. iPhoto is Mac-only and has never had (and likely never will have) a Windows-compatible sister. Once you have the Mac, you'll want to make sure you already have iPhoto '11 on it; if you don't, you'll want to get it (see the earlier "Getting iPhoto '11" section).

For those of you who don't have a Mac that shipped with iPhoto '11 and are upgrading to iLife or iPhoto '11, you'll want to make sure you have a Mac computer with the following:

■ An Intel dual-core processor

■ Mac OS X 10.6.3 or newer (known as "Snow Leopard")

■ At least 1GB of RAM

■ At least 5GB of free hard-drive space

Recommended Extras

Considering the scope of what iPhoto '11 allows you to do, it will also be helpful if you have the following extra items. These are not necessary to use iPhoto, but you'll find having them will allow you to really take advantage of all iPhoto '11 has to offer. You'll learn throughout the book about how having these extras will improve your iPhoto experience.

■ An Internet connection

■ A digital camera

■ An e-mail account

■ A MobileMe account

■ A Facebook account

■ A Flickr account

Keeping iPhoto '11 Up-to-Date

Just because you already have iPhoto '11 on your computer, or have installed iPhoto '11 from a DVD or the Mac App Store in the past, doesn't mean you necessarily have the latest version of iPhoto '11.

Like any good software company, Apple frequently pushes out updates to its applications. These updates typically provide bug fixes or tweaks, but sometimes they even add new functionality to the applications. To make sure you are using the latest version of iPhoto '11, do the following:

1. Go to the Apple menu (🍎) in the upper-right corner of your screen.

2. Select Software Update.

3. Software Update will check for any updates to Mac OS X or any Apple programs, and if it finds any updates, it will list them.

4. If Software Update lists any updates, especially for iPhoto, click the Install button. If there is an iPhoto update, after the update downloads and installs, you'll have the latest version of iPhoto '11.

To check which version of iPhoto you have, open iPhoto and then, from the menu bar at the top of your screen, select iPhoto ➤ About iPhoto. In the box that appears (Figure 1–1) you'll see the version and build number. This number will change from time to time as Apple pushes out iPhoto '11 updates.

Figure 1–1. *The About iPhoto box tells you which version of iPhoto '11 you are using and the build number. Here the version is 9.1.1, and the build number is 527.*

NOTE: You may have noticed that this book refers to the latest version of iPhoto as iPhoto '11. However, when you're looking at the About iPhoto box, it says you have iPhoto 9.*x.x*. So, what's the deal? For marketing purposes, Apple brands the iLife suite by the year. Therefore, iLife '11 contains iPhoto '11, and so on. However, sometimes 18 months will pass without a new iLife suite, which means that there isn't parity between iPhoto version numbers and iLife year numbers. iLife '11 contains iPhoto '11, which is the ninth version of Apple's photo-editing application.

What You'll Need to Know

Now that you've seen what you need to run iPhoto '11 and the extras that help make iPhoto that much more fun and productive, let's talk about the skills you need to possess to use iPhoto.

Don't worry! I'm not talking about photography skills (although I'm sure many of you are excellent photographers). When I say "skills," I'm talking about your computer skills—or more specifically your Mac skills.

Throughout this book I'll assume you have the bare-minimum Mac skills. That is, I'll assume you know how to do the following:

- Turn your Mac on and off
- Open and close Mac applications
- Use a mouse or trackpad
- Use a keyboard
- Use a digital camera
- Know how to plug your digital camera into your Mac's USB port

See? That's all I'll require of you! Easy, huh? You don't need to know a single thing about iPhoto. That's why you have this book!

What Is iPhoto?

Great question! iPhoto is different things to different people. That is to say, it's a very versatile program. Once you learn it, you'll see just how simple Apple has made it to use.

Before I introduce you to the iPhoto interface, let's talk about the three primary things iPhoto allows you to do: organize, edit, and share your photos.

iPhoto Lets You Navigate and Organize Your Photos

Remember the world before digital photography? You'd take photos, go to your grocery store or Walgreens and have them developed, and then return to pick them up. You'd take them out of the envelope and try not to get fingerprint smudges on the glossies. After you looked at them, you might have just put them back in the envelope for safekeeping, or perhaps you were zealous and added all your photos to photo albums. If you were like me, most of the time those photos just ended up in a shoe box.

Digital photography changed a lot of things. You can now see photos as soon as you take them and delete the images you don't like. It eliminated the waiting and printing costs. However, one thing digital photography didn't do at first was help us organize and navigate our photos.

Most of us would plug our digital cameras into our computer and drag all our photos from the camera to a folder on our computer. Perhaps the more organized of us created multiple folders for our photos and took the time to label them. Maybe even a few of us renamed each individual photo, replacing the familiar DSC0240 or IMG_1649 with "Mikes_wedding_001."

Perhaps some of us used the software that came with our cameras. Woe to those who did. The software included with most cameras was often poorly designed, buggy, and more trouble to navigate than just piling the photos into a folder on your hard drive. Even worse, if you bought a new camera and switched brands, say from an Olympus to a Canon, you would often need to change the software program on your computer, since manufacturers designed their photo software to work only with their cameras.

Thankfully, Apple stepped in and created iPhoto. Apple realized that although digital cameras were fun and powerful tools, camera manufacturers weren't as good at designing software as they were at creating phenomenal photography equipment.

Apple designed iPhoto to work with any camera on the market. It lets you easily plug your camera into your Mac and upload your photos in a snap. What's more, iPhoto automatically separates your photos into events, which are collections of photos based on the time you took them. No more piling all your photos into one big folder or library. Furthermore, iPhoto automatically separates your photos into specific albums called Faces and Places, and it lets you navigate through them by person or the location where the photo was taken. I'll talk all about Events, Faces, and Places later in the book.

Apple also understands that users want control over their photo organization and navigation. That's why users can easily merge or add to events, create albums, create folders full of albums, and even create smart albums (albums that have rules applied, such as "Show me all the photos I've rated five stars").

Furthermore, Apple lets users easily search through their photo libraries using iPhoto's powerful Search and Tagging feature.

iPhoto Lets You Edit Your Photos

iPhoto is more than just an organization tool. It's also a powerful photo editor. Using the built-in editing tools, iPhoto can rotate and crop your photos, eliminate red-eye and blemishes with the click of a button, and even straighten crooked pictures.

iPhoto also lets you apply several effects to your photographs, such as lightening or darkening a photo, making it warmer or cooler, and adding sepia tones, vignettes, blurs, and more to photographs.

Finally, iPhoto gives you access to complete histogram tools so you can tweak your photos like a pro. Don't know what a histogram is? You will by the end of this book.

The best of all of iPhoto's editing capabilities is that it uses a nondestructive editor. This means no matter how many times you adjust a photo's color, no matter how many times you crop a photo, and no matter how many times you apply effects, you can always return to the original photo with a click of a button. iPhoto accomplishes this by creating and saving an original copy of your imported photograph every time you begin to edit it. Go ahead and edit a photo 100 times, and then come back to it five years later. Click **Revert to Original**, and the photograph will look as it did the day you took it.

iPhoto Lets You Share Your Photos

Organizing and editing your photos are great features of iPhoto, but let's be honest— many times we don't take photographs solely for our enjoyment. We love to share them with people.

iPhoto allows you to do this through many old-school ways, such as printing a photograph on your printer or e-mailing a photo to a friend. iPhoto also allows you to share your photos in fun and creative new ways.

You can share your photos across the Web via iPhoto's tight social networking integration with Facebook. From within iPhoto you can post entire albums to your Facebook page, tag friends in photos, and even change your profile picture. iPhoto '11 also lets you upload your photos to your MobileMe or Flicker accounts. I'll walk you through all of the web-sharing options later in this book.

iPhoto also mixes the old with the new because it lets you easily design slideshows, calendars, books, and cards right in the program. You can then purchase these items within iPhoto and give them to your friends and family as memory keepsakes.

Launching iPhoto

Unless you have removed it, iPhoto's icon (Figure 1–2) always appears in the Mac OS X Dock at the bottom of your screen. If for some reason the iPhoto icon is not in the Dock, navigate to your Mac HD icon on your desktop, and then go to the Applications folder. You'll find iPhoto there.

Click the iPhoto icon once in the Dock to launch it; double-click it if you are launching iPhoto from within the Applications folder.

Figure 1–2. *The iPhoto icon appears in the Dock or Applications folder.*

The iPhoto '11 Interface

Even if you have previously used other versions of iPhoto, you may feel at a bit of a loss when you open iPhoto '11 for the first time. Apple overhauled the interface and gave it a new layout that helps you take advantage of all the features the program offers.

What's tricky about iPhoto is that the layout of the program changes slightly depending on what you're doing. For example, while you are editing a photo, you'll see different buttons and toolbars than you will when you are organizing your photos or creating a book or card.

I'll show you the complete layouts for all the functions in iPhoto in the appropriate sections of this book. For now, however, check out Figure 1–3, which shows you how iPhoto appears each time you launch the application.

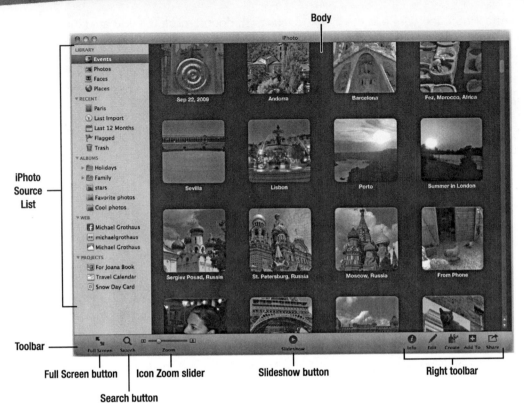

Figure 1–3. *The iPhoto application*

Let's break down the anatomy of the iPhoto program. As you can see, when iPhoto launches, the application is divided into three primary parts: the body, the source list, and the toolbar. That last part, the toolbar, contains the all-important iPhoto tools on the right.

The Main Viewing Area

A majority of the iPhoto application's space is taken up by the main viewing area, or what I call the body. It's the gray space with all the square images in it. In Figure 1–3, the body contains all your events. When in an event, the body will show you all the photos in that event.

As you can imagine, the body changes depending on what function iPhoto is performing. When you are editing, the body will show you the edit screen. When you are creating a calendar, the body will show you the projects screen. I'll talk about all these screens in detail throughout the book.

The Source List

Running down the left side of iPhoto is the source list. You use the source list to easily navigate through all your photos and the way they are organized. This organization includes how you are sharing the photos and any projects you may be working on. The source list in Figure 1–3 is divided into five sections:

■ **Library:** This header comprises four subsections: Events, Photos, Faces, and Places. Select one to navigate your photos using the respective view. You'll learn all about each view later in the book.

■ **Recent:** This header consists of five subsections. The top one, labeled "Paris" in Figure 1–3, shows you the *most recent event* you have viewed. **Last Import** shows you all the photos you imported the last time you connected your camera. **Last 12 Months** shows you all the photos you have imported in the last 12 months. **Flagged** shows you all the photos you have flagged. **Trash** contains all the photos you have deleted from your iPhoto library.

■ **Devices:** This header lists any currently connected cameras, iPods, iPhones, and iPads. I'll talk more about devices in Chapter 2.

■ **Albums:** This header displays all the albums, smart albums, and folders you have created. I'll talk about all of these in Chapter 3.

■ **Web:** If you are using any of the web-based sharing features of iPhoto, such as Facebook, MobileMe, or Flickr, your accounts will show up here.

■ **Projects:** Any projects such as cards, slideshows, books, or calendars that you have or are working on will show up here.

The Toolbar

The toolbar runs along the bottom of iPhoto in the thick gray strip below the source list and the body. It's really divided into two sections, the left and the right. In the left toolbar, you will find the following buttons:

■ **Full Screen:** This allows you to enter iPhoto's cool Full Screen mode. Learn all about it in Chapter 10.

■ **Search:** Click the Search button to find photos by title, keyword, description, date, or rating.

■ **Icon Zoom slider:** Adjust this slider to increase or decrease the size of the event or photo icons in the body.

■ **Slideshow:** Click the Slideshow button to automatically display a slideshow of your currently selected event or photos.

On the right side of the toolbar you'll see five buttons. These buttons are how you access the meatiest features of iPhoto '11. The right side of the toolbar contains the following tools (all which will be discussed in their respective chapters):

- **Info:** Click this to bring up a sidebar that displays detailed information about a selected photo, event, or Faces group. The information can include the camera the photo was taken with, its date and time, a list of people who are in the photo, its GPS coordinates, and keywords and ratings.

- **Edit:** Clicking the Edit button switches iPhoto to edit mode.

- **Create:** This button, whose icon is a pair of scissors and bottle of glue, presents a pop-up menu when clicked, allowing you to create an album, book, card, calendar, or slideshow.

- **Add To:** Clicking the Add To button allows you to add currently selected photos or events to an already existing album, book, card, calendar, or slideshow.

- **Share:** The Share button allows you to share currently selected photos or events with others by uploading them to your MobileMe, Flickr, or Facebook pages or by ordering prints or sending them in the body of an e-mail message.

Summary

This chapter was an overview of the iPhoto application at a glance. It might seem like a lot at first glance, but give it a few chapters, and you'll be using iPhoto like a pro. Before moving forward, you might want to bookmark the page with Figure 1–3 on it for easy reference later.

Also, get ready for some serious fun. iPhoto is one of the best reasons for owning a Mac, and it's going to bring a whole new level of creativity and excitement to your photographic memories.

Importing Your Photos

The first step to using iPhoto is adding pictures to it. After all, a photo-editing and organizing application is pretty useless if you don't have anything to edit or organize. Adding photos to your iPhoto Library is called *importing*. With iPhoto there are several ways you can import your photographs.

In this chapter, you'll learn about all the ways you can import your photographs from various sources including your digital camera, folders on your computer, a photo CD or DVD, a USB flash drive, an iPhone/iPod touch/iPad, and more. Let's get started.

Understanding How iPhoto Handles Imported Photographs

Before you import anything, it's important to understand how iPhoto handles file management of imported photographs. When you import an image into iPhoto, by default it is copied to a specific file on your Mac. This file is called the iPhoto Library and can be found in the **User Name > Pictures** folder on your Mac (see Figure 2–1).

The iPhoto Library file is actually a single database containing all your imported photos organized into a series of folders. These folders preserve the original imported files and also any edits you make. Normally you won't be able to see the individual folders or files inside the iPhoto Library file, but I'll show you a little-known way to explore its contents in Chapter 10, which deals with advanced iPhoto settings and uses.

For now just understand that the advantage of this centralized iPhoto Library file on your computer is twofold:

- It allows you to easily back up your entire photo library by simply copying the iPhoto Library file to an external hard drive.

- It ensures that all the photos on your computer are in one easy-to-find place and eliminates clusters of folders containing pictures being scattered around on your Mac.

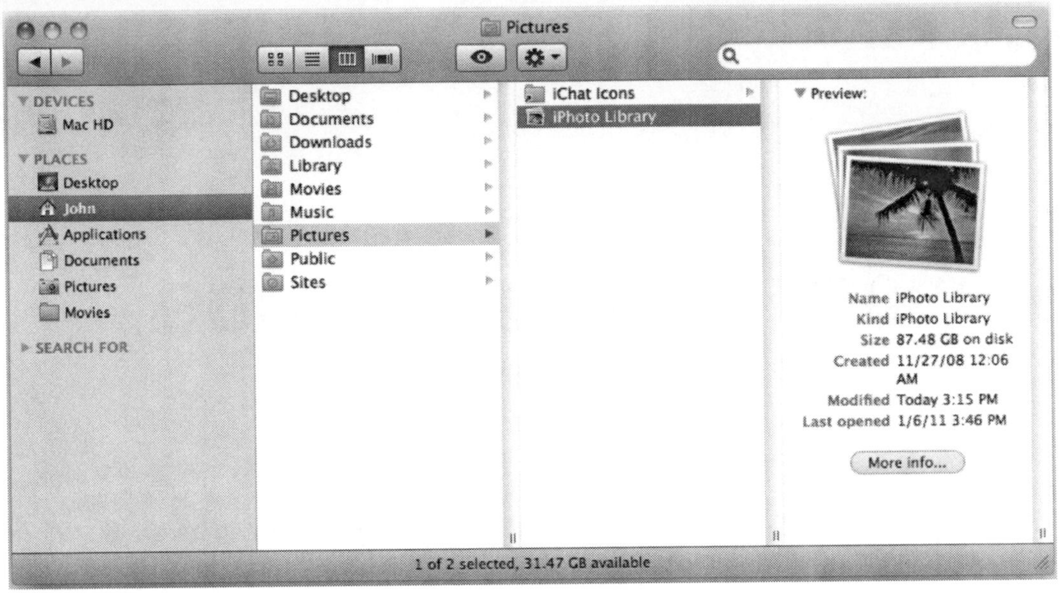

Figure 2–1. *The iPhoto Library file is located in the User Name* ➤ *Pictures folder.*

I mentioned that iPhoto *copies* a photo by default when you add it to your iPhoto Library. This means that, as you'll see shortly, when you drag a photo from the Finder into iPhoto, the original photo will remain in the Finder. The photo that shows up in iPhoto will be a separate copy of that original file. In other words, you'll have two copies of that same photo.

Whether you keep the original copy is up to you. As you'll soon see, after importing a photo from a camera or card reader, you'll be given the option to delete the files from that camera or card reader. iPhoto also gives you the option of turning off the Copy Imported Photos feature in the iPhoto preferences. By turning it off, any photo you import into iPhoto will automatically be removed from its original location and be found only in the iPhoto Library after import.

For the purpose of this book, you'll learn how to use iPhoto with its default settings, but in Chapter 10 I'll walk you through all of iPhoto's preferences and how to change them.

Importing from a Digital Camera or Card Reader

For a majority of you, this will be the primary way you import photographs. Apple knows this, so it made importing from a digital camera or card reader as easy as possible. It used to be that in order to get digital cameras to work with your computer, you needed to install drivers or even entire software suites that came on a CD with the digital camera you bought. Apple recognized that this was confusing for a lot of people, and one of the first big features of iPhoto (and Mac OS X) was the ability to recognize when you had connected a camera without the need to install any plug-ins.

I should note here that no matter if you plug your camera directly into your Mac or if you remove the camera's memory card and plug that into a card reader connected to or built into your Mac, iPhoto will see both the card and the camera as the same device.

By default, when you plug in a camera via the USB port to your Mac or insert a camera card into a card reader that is connected via USB to your Mac, iPhoto will automatically open and ask whether you want to import any photos that are on the camera or card reader. Figure 2–2 shows the screen you'll see when you plug a camera, card reader, or card into your Mac and iPhoto automatically launches.

NOTE: If you have your camera plugged into your Mac and iPhoto does not recognize it, make sure your camera is turned on and that it has battery power. A camera must be powered on and usually be in "view images" mode for iPhoto to recognize it.

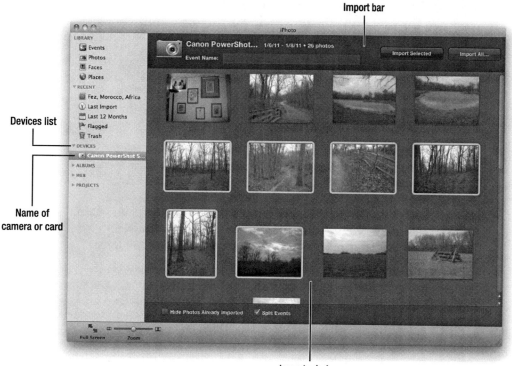

Figure 2–2. *Importing photos into iPhoto from a camera or card*

Figure 2–2 shows you what iPhoto looks like during a general import from your camera or card reader. Let's break down the anatomy of an iPhoto import:

- **Devices heading:** In the source list on the left, you'll see a new heading called Devices has appeared. This heading shows up whenever you have a device connected to your Mac that contains photos that iPhoto can import. Under the Device heading you'll see your camera including its make and model, USB drives, and iPhones, iPod touches, or iPads that contain photos.

  It's important to note that if you insert a photo CD or DVD, it will show up under a Shared heading in iPhoto's source list.

- **Import window:** You'll note that the main body of iPhoto has turned into the Import window. The Import window displays the photos that are currently on your camera.

- **Import bar:** A dark gray bar appears at the top of the Import window. In this bar you'll find an icon and the name of the device currently plugged in (in Figure 2–2 it's a Canon PowerShot camera). Next to that you'll see the date range the photos on the camera were taken during and how many photos are on the camera.

  Below the camera name you'll see a field marked **Event Name**. The **Event Name** field allows you to assign a name to the group of photos you are importing. For example, you might name the photo group "Birthday party" or "Items for eBay sale." The **Event Name** field gives you an easy way to label your various events.

- **Import buttons:** In the Import bar you'll see two buttons. **Import Selected** allows you to import only the photos you have selected in the Import window. In Figure 2–2, the photos with the yellow boxes around them have been selected. Importing only selected photos is handy when you have hundreds of photos on a card and just want to quickly grab a few of them and not wait for the entire import to finish. The **Import All** button imports all the photos on the camera or card.

- **Hide Photos Already Imported:** When selected, this check box at the bottom of the Import window hides any photos on the camera or card that you have previously imported into iPhoto. It's really handy because it lets you quickly eliminate photos from view that you already have in your library.

- **Split Event:** When this box is checked, your imported photos are split into events based on the day they were taken. So, all the photos on the camera roll that you took on Saturday, January 8, are sorted into one event. All the photos from Monday, January 11, are in another event, and so on. I talk all about events in Chapter 4.

Import Steps at a Glance

Now that you understand the anatomy of the Import window, here are the steps you'll need to take to begin an import:

1. Plug in your camera or card reader to your Mac's USB port, or put the card into the Mac's SD card reader.

2. If iPhoto doesn't automatically launch, select it from your Dock or Applications folder.

3. Fill in the event name for your import (optional).

4. Choose whether you want to split events by checking or unchecking the **Split Events** box. This step is optional because you'll likely keep the settings you used the last time.

5. Decide whether you want to import all the photos or select just the ones that you do want to import. To select individual photos, hold down the Command key and click each photo with your mouse, or simply drag a selection box around certain photos by clicking and dragging the mouse button as you move it.

6. Click either the **Import Selected** or **Import All** button to begin your import.

During an Import

Before I continue showing you other ways to import your photographs, let's take a moment to see what happens during an import (see Figure 2–3). This will be the same for most imports no matter what source you are importing your photos from.

Figure 2–3. *The parade of photos during an import*

In Figure 2–3 you can see what happens when you click either the **Import Selected** or **Import All** button. The Import bar changes to show you the progress of your import. The blue progress bar is one indication of how far along your import is. The Import bar also tells you how many photos are left to import. In Figure 2–3 there are 20 photos left to import.

As you import your photos, each appears in the Import window. When one photo is done importing, the next one appears, and so on, until all have been imported. Imports can take a very long time if you have hundreds of photos to add to your library or if the photos are very large.

You can stop a photo import at any time by clicking the **Stop Import** button. Any images that have already been imported show up in your library. The remaining images are still on your camera or card.

After you have completed a successful import, iPhoto gives you the option of deleting or keeping the photos you've just imported (Figure 2–4). To keep the photos on your camera or card, click **Keep Photos**. To delete the photos, click **Delete Photos**.

Figure 2–4. *You can choose to delete the photos you have imported from your camera or card after import.*

I generally delete the photos from my camera as soon as I import them to free up space on my camera's memory card for new pictures. However, there are a few reasons you might want to keep your photos on your camera or card:

- If you're sharing the photos with others and your friends, you may want to import the same photos onto their Mac or PC.

- If your camera or card has enough free space, it never hurts to keep the photos on it because it provides a backup of the photos in your iPhoto Library. However, this option becomes less practical the more photos you shoot.

After a Successful Import: The Last Import Window

Once you choose to keep or delete the photos from your camera, you are taken to the Last Import window (Figure 2–5). **Last Import** is a predefined menu item in iPhoto's source list. You can always find it under the Recent header.

The Last Import window shows you all the photos from your last import, no matter if your last import was three days or three years ago. The photos in the Last Import window are separated into events based on your Autosplit import settings of one event per day, one event per week, or one event per two- or eight-hour gaps. By default iPhoto sets Autosplit settings to one event per day. I'll show you how to change these settings in Chapter 10.

From the Last Import window you can double-click the event's name to rename it. Even though you may have already chosen an event name during the original import process, that name is applied only to the topmost event. Subsequent events must be manually named.

If you have multiple events in the Last Import window, you can drag and drop photos from one event into another here. I go into all the details about events in Chapter 4.

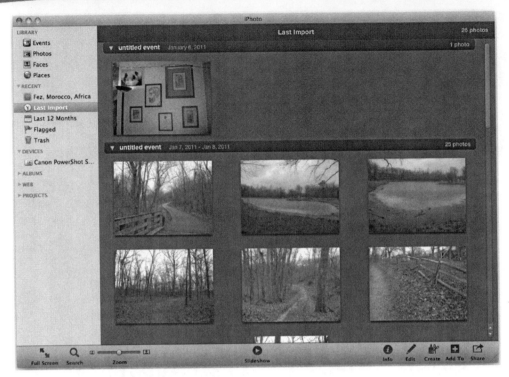

Figure 2–5. *The Last Import window*

Importing from a Folder on Your Mac or from an External Device

Another way you can import photos to iPhoto is directly from your Mac or an external device such as an external hard drive, USB flash drive, CD, or DVD. There are two ways to import photos that are already on your Mac and on external devices.

Using Drag and Drop

The easiest way to import photos that already exist on your Mac or external device is by dragging and dropping them right into iPhoto. Here's how:

1. Select the photo or folder of photos on your Mac or external device.

2. Drag it onto the iPhoto icon in the Dock, or drag it directly into the body of the iPhoto window. The photos are automatically imported and are added to your iPhoto Library.

Keep in mind that the photos have been *copied* to your iPhoto Library. A copy of the photograph still remains in the same place on your Mac or external device that you drug the photos from. You can delete either the original copies or the ones you put into iPhoto without affecting the others.

Using the File Menu

If drag and drop isn't your thing, you can import photos from your Mac or external devices by using the **Import to Library** command from iPhoto's menu bar.

1. From iPhoto's menu bar at the top of your screen, select **File ➤ Import to Library**.

2. In the Import Photos Finder window that appears (Figure 2–6), navigate to the photograph or folder of photos you want to import. These photos could be on your Mac's hard drive or an external hard drive, CD, DVD, or USB flash drive.

3. Select the photos you want to import, and click the **Import** button. Your selected photos are imported to the iPhoto Library.

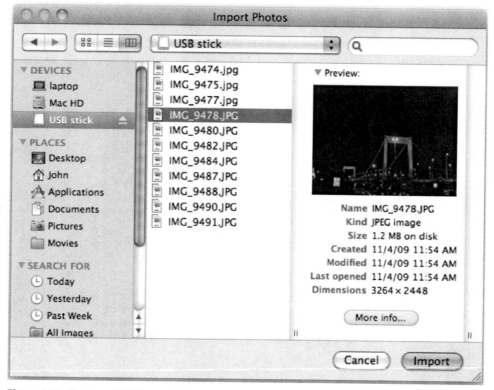

Figure 2–6. *The Import to Library window*

NOTE: When importing photos from your Mac or external devices, iPhoto does not give you the option of deleting the photos from their original source like it does when you import photos from your camera or a memory card.

Saving Photos to iPhoto from Apple's Mail Application

If you use Apple's Mail app as your e-mail client, you can easily save photographs people have e-mailed to you. To do this, follow these steps:

1. Open the Mail app.

2. Select an e-mail with photo attachments.

3. From the e-mail header, click and hold the **Save** button. A drop-down menu appears (see Figure 2–7).

4. From this drop-down menu, select **Add to iPhoto**. The image is successfully added to your iPhoto Library.

Figure 2–7. Saving a photo from Mail to iPhoto

Importing from an iPhone, iPod touch, or iPad

iPhoto works with virtually any digital camera on the market. Unsurprisingly, this includes all of Apple's iOS devices that offer camera functionality such as the iPhone, iPod touch, and iPad.

To import from any of these iOS devices, simply plug your iPhone, iPod touch, or iPad into your Mac via the USB-to-dock cable that came with your iOS device. The iPhone, iPod touch, or iPad appears under iPhoto's Devices header in the source list just as any camera would. Use the same steps as importing from a camera to import from an iPhone, iPod touch, or iPad.

How to Turn Off Automatic iPhone, iPod touch, and iPad Imports

One sticky point when connecting an iPhone, iPod touch, or iPad to your Mac is that iPhoto automatically opens. This can be annoying because you might not necessarily want to import photos each time you plug in your iPhone, iPod touch, or iPad to your Mac. Most of the time you'll be plugging your iOS device into your Mac to charge it or sync new apps to it.

Apple has mysteriously made it difficult to turn off automatic iPhoto launching when you plug in your iOS devices. That doesn't mean there isn't a way to do it. You just need to know where to look.

You would think Apple would have included an option to turn off automatic iPhoto launching when iOS devices are connected in iPhoto's preferences, but Apple didn't. It didn't include the option in the iOS device preferences in iTunes either, which is the primary place you go to set how your iPhone, iPod touch, or iPad works when plugged into your Mac.

Oddly, Apple decided to put this setting in an application called Image Capture (see its icon in Figure 2–8). Image Capture is an advanced application that can be found in your Applications folder on your Mac. It allows you to upload photos from many different sources, such as network drives, scanners, and cameras right to any folder on your Mac. It's also the one place where you can disable iPhoto autolaunching when an iOS device is installed.

Figure 2–8. *The Image Capture icon*

To disable iOS devices from autolaunching iPhoto, do the following:

1. Open Image Capture while your iPhone, iPod touch, or iPad is connected to your Mac.

2. Select your iOS device from under the Devices header in the Image Capture source list (see Figure 2–9).

3. In the box in the lower-left corner of Image Capture, you'll see a drop-down menu labeled **Connecting this iPhone [or iPod touch/iPad] Opens**. By default you'll see that iPhoto is selected.

4. Click where it says iPhoto, and in the drop down-menu select **No Application**.

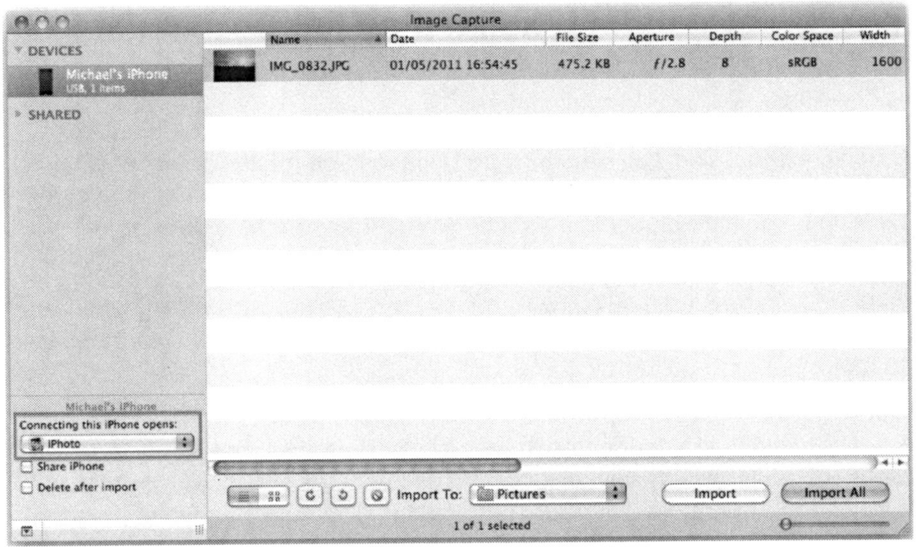

Figure 2–9. *The Image Capture window with the drop-down menu highlighted*

Once you have completed these steps, iPhoto no longer opens automatically every time you connect your iPhone, iPod touch, or iPad. When you do want to import any photos from those devices, you'll simply need to launch iPhoto manually by clicking its icon in the Dock or double-clicking its icon in the Applications folder. Once iPhoto is launched, your connected iPhone, iPod touch, or iPad appears in iPhoto's source list.

Dealing with Duplicates

When importing images from a CD or a folder on your computer, or even from a camera where you left the original images on the card after a prior import, you run the risk of importing photographs you've already imported. Luckily, iPhoto has a built-in duplicate detector. If you should try importing a photograph that you have imported before, the Duplicate Photo warning that you see in Figure 2–10 appears.

The Duplicate Photo warning gives you the option of reimporting the photograph, which adds another copy of it to your library, or not importing it, which causes iPhoto to skip that single photo and move on to the next. If you check the **Apple to All Duplicates** check box, iPhoto either imports all duplicates or doesn't import all duplicates in the current import session, depending on whether you check **Import** or **Don't Import**.

Figure 2–10. *iPhoto's Duplicate Photo dialog box*

Summary

Congratulations! You now know how to import photos from a wide array of sources into iPhoto on your Mac. As you can see, Apple has made it pretty easy to get all of your photos into one centralized location—the iPhoto Library. Now you're all set up to experience the best parts of iPhoto: organizing, editing, and sharing!

In the next chapter, you'll begin learning about specifics for your individual photos such as geotagging, keyword, flagging, rating, and more. Get ready for some serious photo fun!

Marking and Searching Your Photos

When you take a photograph on a digital camera today, you aren't just recording a photo. You're also recording dozens of bits of information about that photo like the lens size, the photo resolution, the name of the camera the photo was taken with, the aperture and shutter speed, the Global Positioning System (GPS) coordinates of the location of the photo, and more.

When you are viewing your photos, this information is of little use. However, when you are organizing and navigating your photos, this information can be invaluable. In this chapter, you'll learn how to easily view all the extra information you recorded when taking your photos as well as how to mark your imported photos by flagging, rating, and adding keywords to them. Finally, I'll show you how your individual photo markups help you search your photo library with ease.

iPhoto's Information Pane

One of iPhoto's great features is the ability to see multiple points of information about a single photo or a group of photos in one convenient location. This location is called the Information pane.

In Figure 3–1 you can see the Information pane on the right side of iPhoto. To access this pane, click the Info button in the iPhoto toolbar at the bottom of the screen. You can also display the Information pane via the menu bar by choosing View ➤ Info or via the keyboard by pressing Command-I.

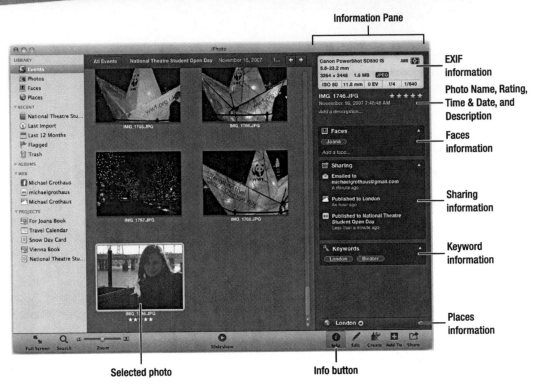

Figure 3–1. *iPhoto's Information pane is displayed on the right side.*

The Information pane gives you a wealth of information about your selected photo. It also displays lots of information for an event or other group of photos. For the purposes of this chapter, I'll touch on the Information pane as it relates to one selected photo. It's easiest to learn it that way. Then when I talk about albums and events later in the book, you'll already be a whiz at recognizing what the Information pane is useful for in respect to photo collections.

In Figure 3–1 you can see I have one photo selected. In the Information pane to the right of the photo, you can see the following:

- **EXIF info:** As you can see, the Information pane displays the EXIF information, or metadata, of your photo, including the photo's name, the rating you give it, the time and date it was taken, and a description for your photo. (EXIF stands for Exchangeable Image File information.)

- **Faces bar:** Below the EXIF information you'll find the Faces bar. Clicking the Faces bar expands it and reveals a list of any faces in your photo. You can also add more faces in this list. I'll talk all about Faces in Chapter 5.

- **Sharing bar:** The Sharing bar shows you where you have shared the selected photo. In Figure 3–1 you can see I've e-mailed the photo, published it to my MobileMe gallery, and published it to a Flickr album. All the ways you can share your photos are explored in Chapter 9.

- **Keywords bar:** The Keywords bar of the Information pane allows you to view and add keywords to your photos. You'll learn all about keywords later in this chapter.

- **Location bar:** The Location bar, when expanded, shows you a Google map with a pin representing the specific location in the world you took your photograph. You're going to want to become a world traveler after you explore all the location features, called Places, of iPhoto in Chapter 6. Note that, for some reason, iPhoto doesn't allow you to have the Location bar expanded while the Faces, Sharing, and Keywords bars are.

What Is EXIF?

Throughout this chapter you'll hear me refer to your photo's EXIF information. What exactly is this? Simply put, Exchangeable Image File information is a file format that records associated information with the photo being shot.

Figure 3–2 shows a close-up of the way EXIF information is displayed in iPhoto's Information pane.

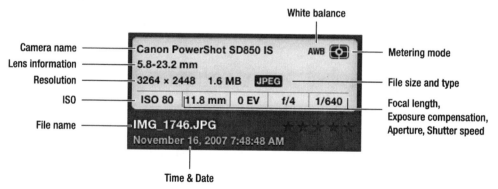

Figure 3–2. *A photo's EXIF information*

Now some of you might see all the numbers in Figure 3–2 and get a little freaked out. Don't worry! You don't need to know what any of the EXIF information means to be a good photographer or enjoy editing and organizing your photos in iPhoto. Apple just added this EXIF information to iPhoto's Information pane for easy reference for those of us who do like to see our photo's EXIF information.

I'll explain what everything means, and if you don't want to worry about this stuff after I do, you don't have to, and you'll be able to enjoy iPhoto as much as the rest of us.

- **Camera name:** This is the name of the camera you took the selected photo with. In this case, it was a Canon PowerShot SD850 IS.

- **White balance:** The letters *AWB* in Figure 3–2 signify that the photo was taken using the camera's automatic white balance. White balancing is a technique that ensures what's white in real life shows up as white when you take a picture of it.

- **Metering mode:** This appears as the crosshairs in a rectangle box in the EXIF window. The metering mode tells you the way your camera determined the photo's exposure.

- **Lens information:** This displays the length of the camera's optical lens. In this case, the camera had a 5.8–23.2mm lens.

- **Resolution:** This shows you the resolution of the photo in pixels. The selected photo is 3264 pixels wide by 2448 pixels high.

- File size: The size of the photo. It's 1.6MB in this case.

- **File type:** The file type of the photo. It's JPEG in this case. Other common formats are TIFF, RAW, and PNG.

- **ISO:** ISO is a measure of how sensitive the image sensor in the camera is to the amount of light present. The higher the ISO, the more sensitive the image sensor is, which increases the ability to take pictures in low-light situations.

- **Focal length:** The focal length determines how much your camera can see. It's the distance between the center of the lens and its focus. In this case, the focal length of the photo is 11.8mm.

- **Exposure compensation:** Basically, exposure compensation allows your camera to automatically brighten or darken images so you can get the best picture possible. A number followed by the letters *EV* designates exposure compensation. In Figure 3–2, the photo's exposure compensation was 0.

- **Aperture:** The aperture is the size of the opening in the camera lens while taking a photograph. This limits the amount of light entering the lens. It is designated by *f/* followed by a number. The higher the number, the smaller the aperture. Higher numbers mean less light. The aperture in the example is f/4.

- **Shutter speed:** This is the length of time the camera's shutter is open. Shutter speed is generally longer in night shots since the length of time the shutter is open must be longer in order to take in the appropriate amount of light. The shutter speed of the photo in the example is 1/640—that means the shutter was open for 1/640th of a second.

- **File name:** Camera manufacturers use conventional standards when naming photos you have taken. These names often begin with "DSC_" or "IMG_"; in Figure 3–2, the name the camera assigned to the photograph is IMG_1746.JPG.

- **Date and time:** Yep, it's the date and time you took your photograph. This is the only EXIF information iPhoto allows you to alter. You'll see how to change this later in this chapter.

Virtually every camera in the world uses the EXIF file format for recording a photo's data. It's a great tool for professional photographers to track their individual shots, but for most iPhoto users, you'll never need to worry about anything you see in the EXIF window again. You know it's there and what it means, and that's enough for now.

Changing Your Photo's Date and Time

As you'll see in upcoming chapters, iPhoto is all about organizing and categorizing your photographs. A big way iPhoto helps you do this is by events (see Chapter 4). For events to work properly, however, your camera must have the correct time and date settings. If it doesn't, when you search through your events, you may see photos that you took last week show up chronologically in the past, way behind photos you took years ago.

Why might your photos not show the correct date and time? Usually it's because your camera's internal battery ran out of juice. Other causes could be that you never set the correct date and time in the first place or, during long distance trips, you haven't changed your camera's time settings to reflect the date and time of the time zone you were in.

To change a single photo's date and time, follow these steps:

1. Select the photo so a yellow box highlights its edges.

2. From the menu bar select Photos ➤ Adjust Date and Time.

   The dialog box in Figure 3–3 appears. You'll see the photo you have selected as well as the original date and time.

3. In the **Adjusted** field, enter the new date and time you want to select for the photo. In the dialog box you'll see by how much the original date and time will be changed.

4. Select the **Modify Original Files** box if you want to change the date and time to the photo's original file in your iPhoto Library file. This step is optional. Selecting this box changes the embedded EXIF date data. If you don't select this box, the original EXIF data stays the same, and the date change affects the photo only while in your iPhoto Library.

5. Click the **Adjust** button, and the change is made. The new date and time are reflected in the photo's Information pane.

Figure 3–3. *Changing a single photo's date and time*

You aren't limited to changing the date and time of one photo at a time. You can change the date and time for an entire event or a group of photos.

To change the dates and times of an event or a group of selected photos, follow these steps:

1. Select the event so a yellow box highlights it. If you are selecting multiple photos, make sure all of the ones you want to change are highlighted.

2. From the menu bar select **Photos ➤ Adjust Date and Time**.

   The dialog box in Figure 3–4 appears. You'll see the first photo of the event or group of photos you have selected as well as the first photo's original date and time.

3. In the **Adjusted** field, enter the new date and time you want to select for the *first* photo. iPhoto uses this date and time to adjust all the other photos accordingly. So, if you change the first photo's time by adding 37 minutes to it, all the photos that you have selected to change will have 37 minutes added to their times. In the dialog box you'll be shown by how much the original date and time will be changed.

4. Check the **Modify Original Files** box if you want to change the date and time to the photos' original files in your iPhoto Library file. This step is optional. Selecting this box will change the embedded EXIF date data. If you don't select this box, the original EXIF data stays the same, and the date change affects only the photos while in your iPhoto Library.

5. Click the **Adjust** button, and the change will be made. The new dates and times will be reflected in the photo's Information pane.

Figure 3–4. *Changing multiple photos' dates and times*

You can also use the **Batch Change** menu item to change multiple photos' dates and times. I'll discuss batch changing later in this chapter.

Changing Your Photo's Name and Adding a Description

iPhoto gives you the ability to replace the boring file names your camera gives your photographs (like *IMG_1746.JPG*) to anything you want. If you have tens of thousands of photographs, renaming each one might get tedious, but being able to name individual photos can be very helpful for your favorites, especially when it comes to searching through your library.

It's important to note that though I'm using the terms *name* or *file name*, iPhoto doesn't actually let you change the file name of the photo that is stored in the photo's EXIF data. That data is unchangeable. When you change the file name of a photo in iPhoto, you are effectively replacing the name or title iPhoto has given the image (the EXIF file name) with one of your choosing.

To change a photo's name/title, follow these steps:

1. Select the photo so a yellow box highlights it.

2. From the Information pane, double-click the photo's file name. It will change to a text entry field (Figure 3–5).

3. Type any name you want, and press the Return key on your keyboard to finalize it.

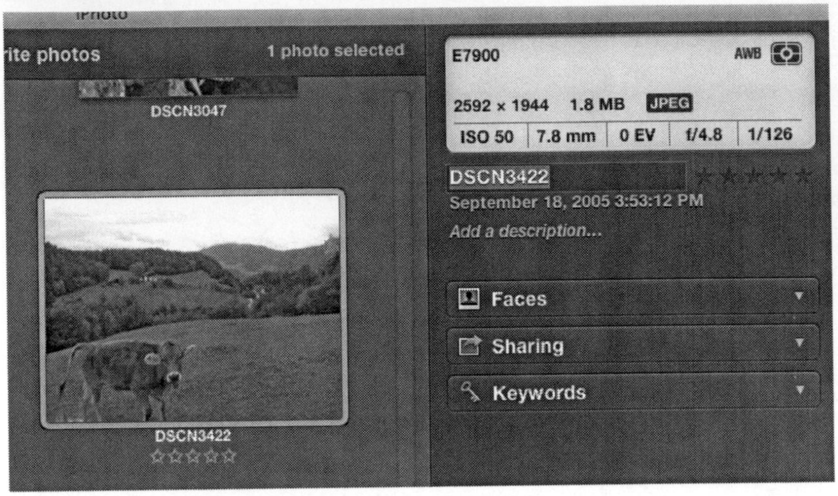

Figure 3–5. *Changing a photo's name*

You can also double-click the name of the photo directly under the photo to change it. You won't see the photo's name underneath it unless you've selected View ➤ Titles from the menu bar.

iPhoto also lets you add a description to your individual photos. Descriptions are cool because you can record a little blurb about each photo—something to help you remember it by. Descriptions are also helpful when you are searching your iPhoto Library, as you'll find out later in this chapter.

To add a description to a photo, follow these steps:

1. Select the photo so a yellow box highlights it.

2. From Information pane, double-click the **Add a Description** text. It will change to a text entry field (Figure 3–6).

3. Type any description you want. Click outside the text field to finalize it. Note that only the first two lines of description are visible, but if you hover your mouse over it, the entire description will pop up in a semi-transparent box.

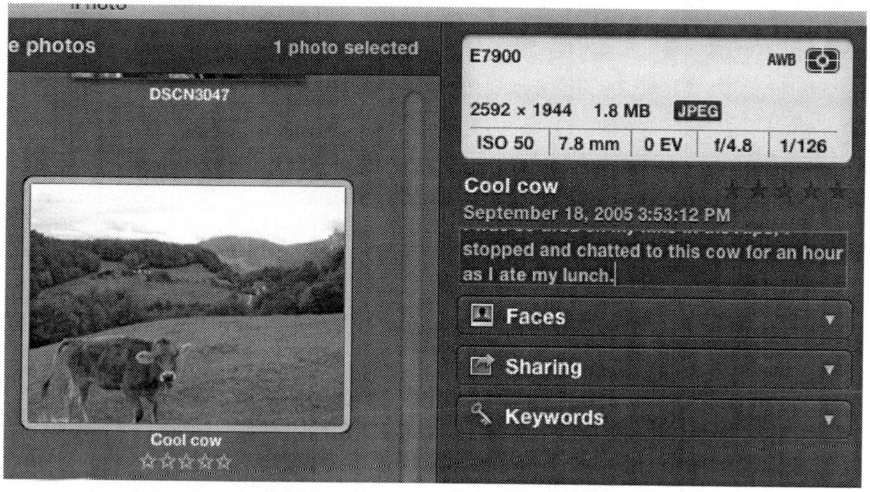

Figure 3–6. *My friend, the cow; adding a description to a photo*

Batch Changing Titles, Dates, and Descriptions

iPhoto offers a Batch Change feature if you find you have hundreds and hundreds of photos to add similar titles, dates, or descriptions to. To use the Batch Change feature, follow these steps:

1. Select the photos or event so a yellow box highlights them.

2. From the menu bar at the top of your screen select Photos ➤ Batch Change.

3. A drop-down menu will appear allowing you to select what you want to batch change: Title, Date, or Description. Select the appropriate one.

   ▪ For Title you'll be able to set the following:

      ▪ **Empty:** Clears any previous title name from the photographs.

      ▪ **Text:** Any text you enter in the text field will become the photos' titles. You can check Append a Number to Each Photo to add a sequential number after each one. For example, if you title the photos as "Cool," all the images selected will be named "Cool – 1," "Cool – 2," and so on.

      ▪ **Event Name:** This assigns the name of the photo's event as the photo's title.

      ▪ **Filename:** This changes the photos' names to their individual file names from their EXIF data.

      ▪ **Date/Time:** This changes the titles of each photo to the photos' dates and times.

- For **Date** you'll be able to enter the data and time you want the photos to have. You can then check the **Add** box and incremental time between each photo by the second, minute, hour, or day.

- For **Description** you can enter a short description into the text box. If you check the **Append to Existing Description** box, the Batch Change description will be added to any existing descriptions.

4. Click the **OK** button to finalize the batch change.

Adding Keywords to Your Photos

Remember how you used to flip a photo over and write on its backside who was in it or maybe where it was taken or what the event was? A digital photo has no such backside, but Apple still lets you amend labels to it. This feature is called *keywords*.

A keyword is simply a tag or label that you apply to your photographs. These tags come in handy when you are searching for specific photos.

To add a keyword to a photo or group of photos (see Figure 3–7), follow these steps:

1. Select the photos or group of photos to which you want to add a keyword. You can also select an event to add keywords to. A keyword that's added to an event is added to every photo in the event.

2. Click the **Info** button in the button bar at the right side of iPhoto's screen to open the Information pane.

3. In the Information pane, click the Keywords bar to expand the Keywords section of the Information pane. Click where you see **Add a keyword**, and then type your keywords into the **Keywords** field.

4. Press Return after each keyword. This separates one keyword from the next. A completed keyword is enclosed in a little pill-shaped oval.

You can add as many keywords to an event or photo as you like. To delete a keyword from a photo or event, simply select the keyword in the Keywords bar and press your Delete key.

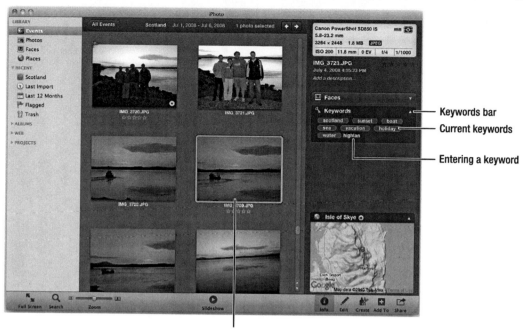

Keywords bar

Current keywords

Entering a keyword

Selected photo

Figure 3–7. *Adding keywords to a photo*

The Keyword Manager

Sometimes it's easy to go a bit overboard while adding keywords. For example, if you have a photo of a dog, it's easy to start tagging it with every dog reference you know: "dog," "puppy," "hound," "mutt," and so on.

If you ever want to see all the keywords you've created and have the option of editing them, you can find them all in the Keyword Manager, as shown in Figure 3–8.

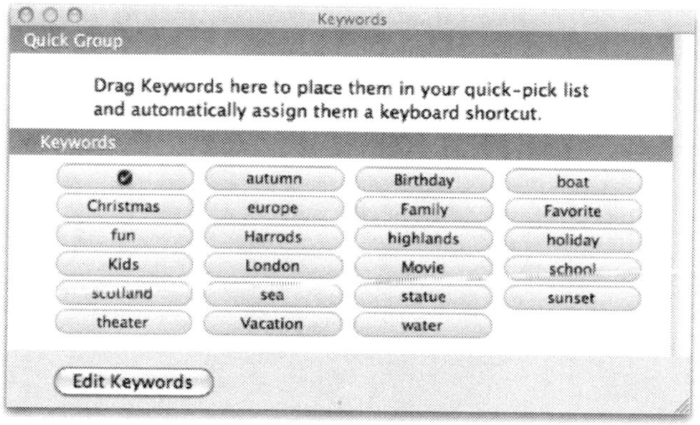

Figure 3–8. *iPhoto's Keyword Manager*

To access the Keyword Manager, from iPhoto's menu bar select **Window ➤ Manage my Keywords**. Alternately, you can pull up the Keyword Manager using the Command-K shortcut key.

In the Keyword Manager that appears you'll see all the keywords you have already added to your photos. You'll also notice some existing keywords Apple has added, such as "Kids" and "Birthday."

From this Keyword Manager you can create, edit, delete, and assign shortcut keys to your keywords.

Creating, Editing, and Deleting Keywords

Each time you label a photo with the steps I outlined previously, that keyword is added to your keyword store automatically. In other words, you've created a keyword.

Another way to create keywords without having to apply them to photos at the time is through the Keyword Manager. With the Keyword Manager open, select **Edit Keywords**. The window you see in Figure 3–9 appears.

- To add a keyword, click the + button, and enter the new keyword in the field that appears.

- To delete a keyword, select the keyword from the list, and click the – button. A window will appear asking "Are you sure you want to remove the selected keyword?" Below this message you'll see how many photos will be affected if you remove the keyword. Deleting a keyword removes that keyword from all the photos that contain it in your iPhoto Library. Click **OK** to delete the keyword.

- To edit a keyword, double-click the keyword, and enter your edit in the text field. Editing a keyword is handy if you've labeled hundreds of photographs with a misspelled keyword. Deleting that misspelled keyword would remove it from all the photos, which means you'd have to go back and retag them with a newly created (and properly spelled) keyword. Editing a keyword allows you to fix spelling mistakes and have it automatically apply to all the photos that contain the existing keyword.

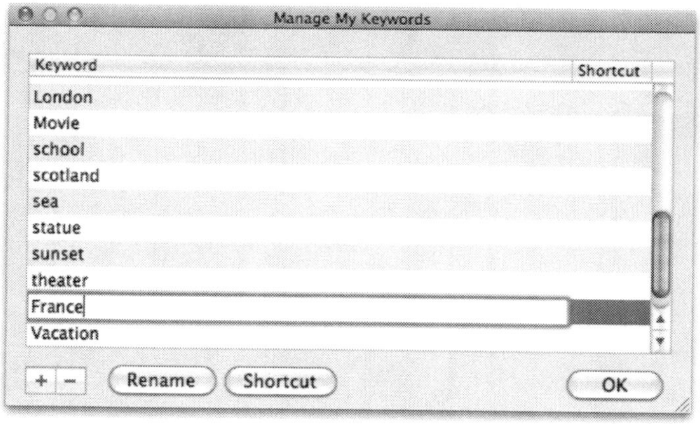

Figure 3–9. *Adding, editing, and deleting keywords*

Adding Keyboard Shortcut Keys to Keywords

Keywords are a terrific tools; however, adding them to many, many photographs can get rather tedious if you have to repeatedly go through the steps I've outlined previously. An easier way to quickly add keywords to your photographs is by assigning keyboard shortcuts to your keywords.

To add keyboard shortcuts to your keywords, follow these steps:

1. From iPhoto's menu bar select Window ➤ Manage my Keywords.

2. Click **Edit Keywords**.

3. Select a keyword you want to create a shortcut for, and click the **Shortcut** button.

4. Enter a letter representing that keyword in the shortcut field. Usually it's a good idea to use the first letter of the keyword. If a letter is already taken by another keyword, you'll have the option of choosing which keyword you want to use the letter with (Figure 3–10).

5. Click OK when you are done adding shortcuts.

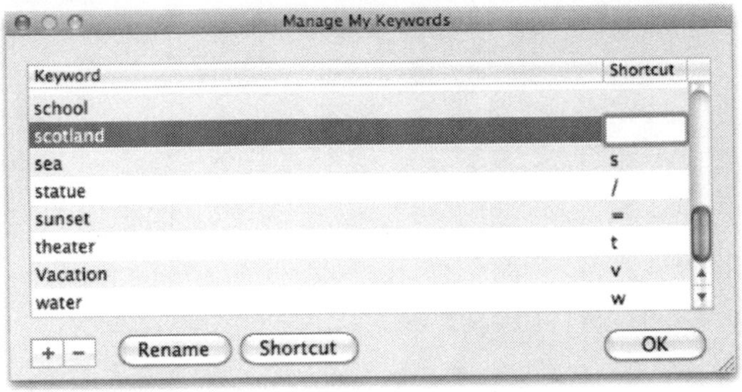

Figure 3–10. *Adding keyboard shortcuts for keywords*

NOTE: You can use any letter, number, or punctuation key on the keyboard as a keyword shortcut. You cannot, however, use symbols or punctuations that use a modifier key (for example, you cannot use the dollar sign because typing it requires you to press Shift+4).

When you click OK and return to the Keyword Manager, you'll notice that any keywords that have shortcut keys applied to them show up under the Quick Group heading (see Figure 3–11). Next to the keyword you'll see its shortcut key enclosed in a gray circle.

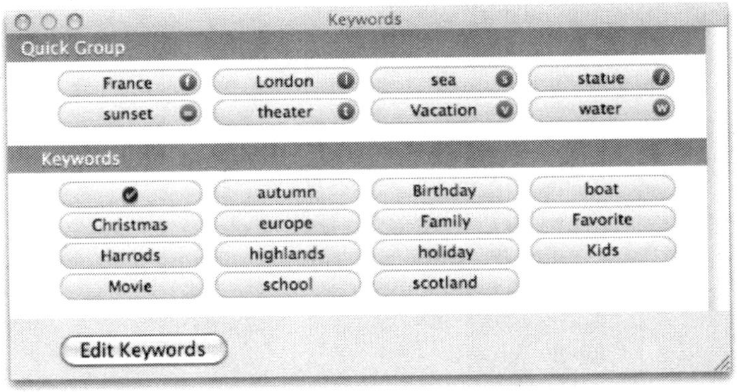

Figure 3–11. *Keywords with shortcut keys show up under the Quick Group list*

From the Keyword Manager you can drag and drop keywords between the Quick Group and Keywords headings. Placing a keyword from the Quick Group heading into the Keywords heading group removes its shortcut key.

Placing a keyword from the Keywords heading into the Quick Group heading group automatically adds a shortcut key to the keyword. The automatically added shortcut key will be the first letter of the word. If that letter is already taken, the second letter of the keyword will be used, and so on.

Applying Keywords Using Keyboard Shortcut Keys

Now that you have your keyboard shortcuts assigned to keywords, you can quickly assign keywords to your photos. Here's how:

1. From iPhoto's menu bar select **Window ➤ Manage My Keywords**.

2. Move the Keyword Manager window aside so you can see your photograph in iPhoto.

3. Now simply select your photographs and press the appropriate shortcut key to assign that specific keyword to the photo or group of photos.

4. Close the Keyboard Manager when you are done assigning keywords.

If you do a lot of keyword tagging, you'll quickly come to realize the speed advantages of assigning keywords using keyboard shortcuts.

Flagging Your Photos

Similar to how adding keywords to photos duplicates the experience of writing words down on the back of old paper photographs, flagging your photos in iPhoto is the equivalent of placing a selected photo to the side in its own special pile while you browse the rest of your photos.

When you flag a photo in iPhoto, it is added automatically into a special Flagged photo album that always exists under the Recents header in iPhoto's source list (Figure 3–12).

- **To flag a photo:** Select the photo or photos and click the Flag Indicator in the photos' upper-left corner, or select the photo or photos and choose **Photos ➤ Flag Photo** from iPhoto's menu bar. The photos are added to the Flagged photo album automatically. The flag indicator will not appear in the corner of a photo until you move your mouse over it.

- **To unflag a photo:** Select the already flagged photo or photos and click the Flag Indicator in the photos' upper-left corner, or select the already flagged photo or photos and choose **Photos ➤ Unflag Photo** from iPhoto's menu bar. The photos are removed from the Flagged photo album automatically.

- **To unflag all flagged photos:** Select the Flagged album from the source list and then click the **Clear Flagged** button at the top of the album, or hover your mouse over the flagged photos number indicator in the source list and click the X that appears.

So, why flag a photo? Here are some of the times I do it:

- When I'm deciding to delete some photos, I pull the redundant ones out so I can review them later.

- When I'm selecting photos for a project, such as a calendar or book, I flag them so I can easily group photos from across events and albums into one quick list—the Flagged album.

- When I'm selecting photos from across multiple events or albums to combine into one event or add them to another album, I flag them.

- When I'm thinking about ordering prints of some photographs or choosing which ones to print myself, I flag them.

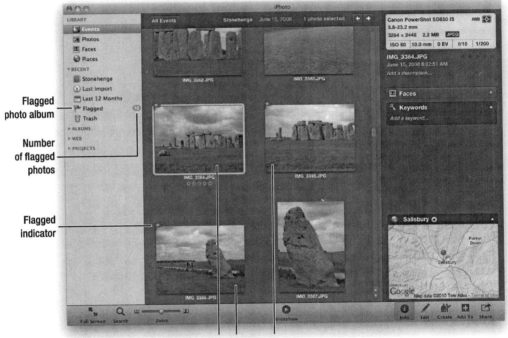

Figure 3–12. *Flagged photos in an event are automatically added to the flagged album in iPhoto's source list.*

Rating Your Photos

iPhoto allows you to assign ratings to your photos so you can record how much you like each one. iPhoto's rating system is based on zero to five stars. Rating your photos isn't just something you do to pass the time. Rating them can help you easily search through your library or create photo albums based on your ratings.

You have five ways to rate your photos. Like most other marking options in iPhoto, you can rate one photo at a time or group multiple photos together to rate them. Figure 3–13 shows you four of the ways you can rate your photos. First, select the photo or photos you want to rate; then you can do one of the following:

- **From iPhoto's menu bar:** Select Photos ➤ My Rating and choose None or one to five stars.

- **From your keyboard:** Press the Command key on your keyboard and then 0, 1, 2, 3, 4, or 5 to rate the selected photos between 0 and 5 stars.

- **From iPhoto's Info Pane:** Click and drag your mouse over the hollow stars to rate the photo.

- **From underneath a photo:** Click and drag your mouse over the hollow stars to rate the photo. To view ratings underneath photos, you must make sure you have selected View ➤ Ratings from the menu bar.

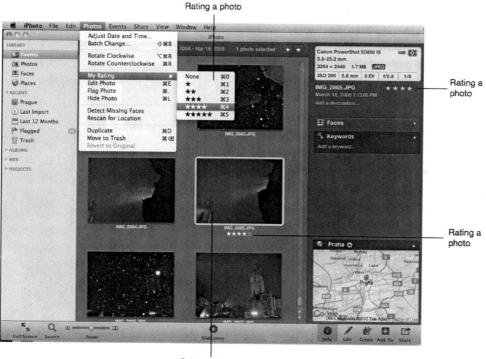

Figure 3–13. *There are several ways to rate your photographs in iPhoto.*

A fifth way to rate your photos is via a contextual menu. I'll discuss this contextual menu in its own section later in the chapter.

Hiding Your Photos

iPhoto gives you the ability to hide certain photos of your choosing. I know, all your photos are amazing, so why would you want to hide any of them? Hiding is useful when you are thinking about deleting a photo but aren't quite sure if you want to do that. In the meantime, choosing to hide it removes it from view in your iPhoto Library.

To hide a photo, follow these steps:

1. Select the photo or photos you want to hide.

2. From the menu bar select **Photos ➤ Hide Photo**.

3. The photos will be removed from viewing, and at the top of iPhoto's window you will be notified of how many photos are hidden in the particular album or event or in Faces or Places.

To view hidden photos, select **View ➤ Hidden Photos** in the menu bar. This does not unhide the photos because they are still marked as hidden. This simply shows you all the photos you have hidden. Hidden photos in this view are marked with an orange X in their upper-right corners (see Figure 3–14).

If you select **View ➤ Hidden Photos** again, the photos you have marked as hidden will vanish from view again.

Figure 3–14. *Viewing a hidden photo. Note the orange X in the corner.*

To unhide a photo, follow these steps:

1. Select **View ➤ Hidden Photos** in the menu bar so you can see all the photos you have hidden.

2. Select your hidden photos, and choose **Photos ➤ Unhide Photo** from the menu bar.

Deleting Your Photos

Sometimes you are going to decide to delete some of your photographs. This can be for several reasons. Perhaps the shot is blurry. Maybe the photo is similar to dozens of others you've taken of the same thing. Whatever your reason, you want to get rid of it. Here's how:

1. Select the photo or photos you want to delete.

2. Press the Delete key on your keyboard, or choose Photos ➤ Move to Trash from the menu bar.

3. A dialog confirmation box will appear asking you to confirm you want to move the photo to the trash. Click the OK button.

At this point, you haven't actually deleted your photos from iPhoto yet. You've just moved them to iPhoto's trash can. iPhoto's trash can icon can always be seen in the source list (Figure 3–15). Hovering your mouse over the trash icon displays a small window that shows you how many photos you have in the trash.

Figure 3–15. *iPhoto's trash can*

> **NOTE:** Moving a photo to iPhoto's trash removes that photo from all albums, events, and projects that photo appeared in, including any books, cards, or calendars you may have created. If you shared the photo online via Flickr, MobileMe, or Facebook, it will remain there until you remove it.

If you've changed your mind and don't want to delete your photos or a few select photos you've moved to the trash, you can choose to restore your photos to your iPhoto Library.

To restore a photo from the trash, follow these steps:

1. Select the photo or photos.

2. Choose **Photos ➤ Restore to Library** from the menu bar.

Once you have done this, your photos are placed back in the albums, events, and projects in which they were located before you moved them to the trash.

To permanently delete the photos from your library, follow these steps:

1. Select **Trash** in the source list, and click the **Empty Trash** button.

2. A dialog box appears asking whether you are sure you want to delete the photos permanently. Click **OK**.

Now *technically* at this point you have deleted the photos from your iPhoto Library file on your computer.

However, until you empty your computer's trash can by choosing **Finder ➤ Empty Trash**, your photos will remain on your computer, albeit in the trash can. Once you empty your computer's trash, your deleted photos are really, truly gone forever unless you have backed them up. We talk about backing up your photo library in Chapter 10.

The Contextual Menu

Many of the operations I've reviewed in this chapter can also quickly be accessed by using a contextual menu built into iPhoto. To access this contextual menu, move your mouse over a photograph, and click the tiny downward-facing arrowhead that appears in the lower-right corner. The contextual menu you see in Figure 3–16 will appear. Optionally, you can right-click anywhere on the photo to bring up its contextual menu.

Figure 3–16. *A photo's contextual menu options*

From this contextual menu, you can do the following:

- **Rotate:** Click this arrow to rotate the selected photo counterclockwise 90 degrees at a time. This is great for easily fixing photos so they appear right way up in the iPhoto Library.

- **Hide:** This is another way to hide a photo. Simply click the orange X.

- **Trash:** Click the trash can icon to move the photo to iPhoto's trash.

- **Rating stars:** Click and drag your mouse over these stars to rate the photo.

- Cut, Copy, Paste: These cut or copy the selected photo or paste a previously copied photo.

- **Make Key Photo:** This makes the selected photo an event's key photo. I'll talk about key photos and events in Chapter 4.

Searching Your Photos

iPhoto offers you powerful search capabilities. It allows you to search your photos using many of the things you have learned about in this chapter as parameters, including photo names and descriptions, EXIF information such as dates, and keywords and ratings.

Before you begin your search, it is important to note that if you know where the photo that you are looking for might be located, such as in a certain event or album, select that event or album before clicking the Search button, as shown in Figure 3–17. Doing so will narrow down the location iPhoto searches for photos. To search your entire library, select Events or Photos from iPhoto's source list.

Search button

Figure 3–17. *iPhoto's Search button*

When you click the Search button in iPhoto's button bar at the bottom of the screen, it changes to a **Search** field (Figure 3–18). Inside this **Search** field you'll see a search menu icon that looks like a magnifying glass. Click this icon to choose from four search options: All, Date, Keyword, and Rating.

Search options

Search menu   Search field

Figure 3–18. *The Search field and search pop-up menu options*

Searching by Text

Apple really should have named the **All** search menu option Text because that's what it does—it allows you to search for text associated with a photo, including names, keywords, and descriptions.

To search for photos by text, follow these steps:

1. Click the **Search** button in the iPhoto button bar.

2. In the **Search** field enter the text you want to find.

3. As you enter text, the body of iPhoto's window populates with those photos matching your inputted text.

iPhoto's search is dynamic. That means if you start typing in *HOLIDAY* one letter at a time, photos with the letters *HO* such as "Holland" will appear alongside photos with the words "holiday" associated with them. When you type in *HOLI*, those photos labeled "Holland" will disappear, yet those labeled "Holiday" will remain.

4. To clear the search field of text, click the *X* on the right side of the search field.

Searching by Date

To search for photos by date, follow these steps:

1. Click the **Search** button in the iPhoto button bar.

2. From the **Search** field menu, click **Date**, and a calendar pop-up with the year and months appears (Figure 3–19).

3. Navigate the years by clicking the left and right arrows in the pop-up menu.

Months that are grayed out have no photos taken during that time in your iPhoto Library. Months in white have associated photos taken during that time. To view photos taken during any given month, click the month name.

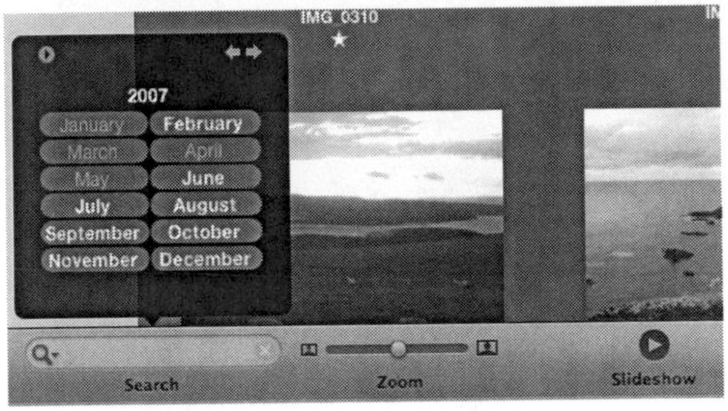

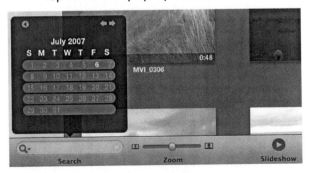

Figure 3–19. *Search by date in month view.*

4. To search for photos on a specific day of the month, double-click the month. A daily calendar will appear (Figure 3–20). You can also access the daily calendar view by clicking the arrowhead in the circle at the top left of the pop-up menu.

5. From this daily calendar you can click a specific date to see the photos taken on that date only. To return to the month view, click the arrowhead in the circle at the top left of the pop-up menu.

Figure 3–20. *Search by date in day view.*

Searching Multiple Dates

iPhoto allows you to search a range of dates or a group of nonconsecutive dates.

To search a range of dates, follow these steps:

1. In either the month or day calendar view, click the beginning month or date.

2. Navigate through the calendar until you find your ending date range.

3. Click the ending date while holding down the Shift key.

4. iPhoto displays all the photos taken in the date range you selected.

To search multiple, nonconsecutive dates, follow these steps:

1. Select the first month or day you want to begin searching on.

2. Select additional months or days while holding down the Command key.

3. iPhoto displays all the photos taken on the nonconsecutive dates you selected.

Searching by Keywords

Now that you are getting familiar with iPhoto's search functions, I hope you can see why keywords can be a powerful search tool. To search by keywords, follow these steps:

1. Click the **Search** button in the iPhoto button bar.

2. From the **Search** field menu, click **Keyword**, and a list containing all your keywords will appear as a pop-up menu (Figure 3–21).

3. If you hover your mouse over a keyword in the list, you'll see a number displayed that shows you just how many photos are tagged with that keyword. To view those photos, click the keyword, and they'll appear in iPhoto's body. Note that the clicked keyword button turns to white.

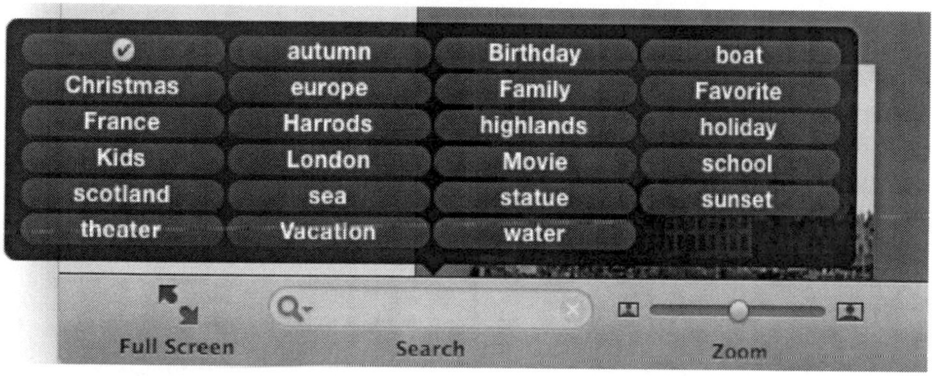

Figure 3–21. *Search by keywords.*

4.   If you click another keyword, it also changes into a white button. Clicking two or more keywords shows you only the photos with *all* of those keywords in them. To search for photos using a single keyword, make sure you click any white keyword buttons to deselect them.

Advanced Keyword Searching

iPhoto has some pretty nifty advanced keyword searching features built in. iPhoto lets you use keyboard keys as "logical operators." In other words, you can search for photos containing some keywords but exclude those same photos from your search results if they contain certain keywords as well.

Let's say you have lots of photos labeled "water." Some of these water photos show pictures of flood damage to your basement (which you've tagged using the keywords "water," "house," "insurance," and "flood"). Others show the lake you vacationed at in Missouri last summer (keywords: "water," "vacation," "lake," "summer," "US"). Still others show pictures you took at of the Mediterranean Sea (keywords: "water," "sea," "vacation").

So, you're searching for all your photos that contain water, but you want to exclude the pictures of the flood damage to your house. Use the following logical operator keys to construct the keyword search:

Shift key = "OR."

Option key = "NOT."

Control key = "And."

1.   Click the Search button in the iPhoto button bar.

2.   From the Search field menu, click Keyword, and a list containing all your keywords appears as a pop-up menu.

3.   Click the keyword "water." The pictures of your flooded basement, the lake, and the Mediterranean appear.

4.   Then, click the keyword "flood" while holding down the Option key. This eliminates all the photos from the "water" search that also contain the keyword "flood." Now you're just left with the pictures of the lake and the Mediterranean. This inspires you to create a book to showcase your vacation photos, and you remember that you got some good pictures of some mountains in southern Poland.

5.   Holding down the Control key, click the keyword "Mountain." This tells iPhoto you want to search for all photos containing "water," and "mountain" but not "flood."

6.   It takes a bit to get your head wrapped around keyword operators, but once you do, you'll like searching with them.

Searching by Ratings

The last way to search your photos is by ratings. This is my favorite way because it's the simplest and also quickly shows you your favorite snapshots. There are two ways to search using ratings: inclusive and exclusive.

- **Inclusive:** If you do an inclusive ratings search for, say, four stars, iPhoto will show you all the photos with *at least* a four-star rating. Since five-star rated photos contain four stars, you'll see them too.

- **Exclusive:** An exclusive rating search shows you only the photos with the exact number of stars you enter. So if you search for three-star photos, you will not see four- or five-starred photos.

To search by exclusive ratings (Figure 3–22), follow these steps:

1. Click the **Search** button in the iPhoto button bar.

2. In the **Search** field, use your keyboard to enter the number of stars you want to see rated photos for. Do this by pressing Shift-8 to create asterisks. You can enter up to five asterisks (representing five stars).

3. iPhoto populates the matching photos in your window.

4. Only the photos with the exact number of rating stars are shown.

Figure 3–22. *Search by exclusive ratings. In this image I have searched for all photos rated only four stars. Only photos with a four-star rating will be shown.*

To search by inclusive ratings, follow these steps:

1. Click the **Search** button in the iPhoto button bar.

2. From the **Search** field menu, click **Rating**, and five hollowed-out stars appear in the **Search** field (Figure 3–23).

3. Click and drag your mouse over the stars to select what rating you want to search for.

4. Photos containing the star rating or higher that you entered are displayed.

Figure 3–23. *Search by inclusive ratings. In this image I have searched for all photos rated at least four stars. This includes four- and five-star photos.*

Summary

By now you know how to read iPhoto's Information pane, which contains very important data about your photographs. Some of this data, such as the EXIF data, is unchangeable, but the Information pane also shows you various markups you've applied to your photos such as naming, descriptions, and keywords—all of which you can edit to your liking. It also shows you how you are sharing your photos (which I talk about in Chapter 9), who's in them (Faces, Chapter 5), and where they were taken (Places, Chapter 6).

Finally, you learned how to search through your photo library, which is a very handy feature for those of you who have tens or even hundreds of thousands of photos.

Navigating and Organizing Your Photos: Events and Albums

With all the photos people take with their digital cameras nowadays, it's sometimes hard to remember when you used to say "Oh, I wish I would have taken the photo from *that* angle." The great thing about digital photos is, of course, unlike older film cameras, that we can take as many photos as we want. This glut of photos, however, can make organizing and navigating them a chore.

Luckily, no matter whether you're the organized type or the "let things fall where they may" type, iPhoto lets you keep your photos organized with zero effort on your part. It does this by using the Events feature. For those of you who *do* like organizing your photographs, however, iPhoto offers you the option of sorting your photos in albums and smart albums.

In this chapter, you'll learn how to organize and navigate your photos using events, albums, and smart albums.

Events

So, what is an event exactly? It's a collection of your photographs that spans a certain timeframe, automatically grouped by iPhoto upon import from your camera. By default, every time you import photos from your camera, iPhoto will sort them into events based on the day they were taken.

Autosplitting Events

iPhoto calls this sorting of your photos *autosplitting*. So if you import photos that were taken over a period of three days, iPhoto sorts, or autosplits, those photos into three separate events.

You can change iPhoto's default autosplitting timeframe by navigating to **iPhoto ➤ Preferences** in the menu bar and selecting the General tab (Figure 4–1). From the **Autosplit into Events** drop-down menu, you can choose to have iPhoto split imported photos into events by one event per day, into events by one event per week, or into two-hour or eight-hour gaps.

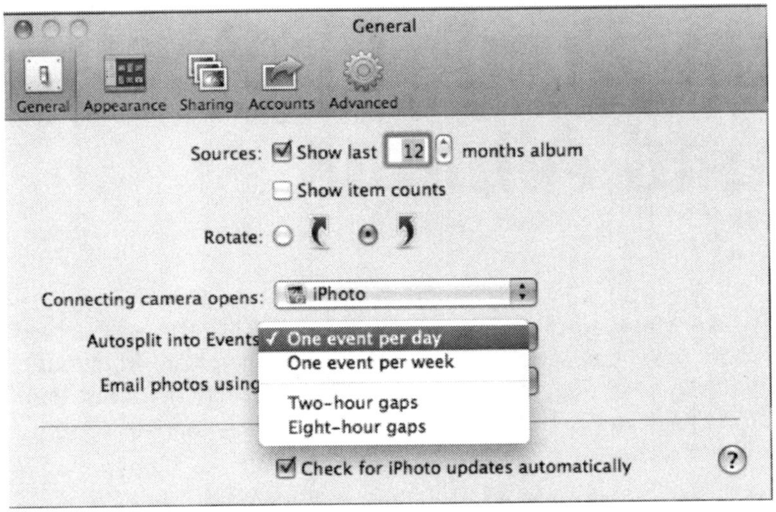

Figure 4–1. *Setting iPhoto's autosplit preference for events*

Changing events' autosplitting time window from one event per day to two- or eight-hour gaps is handy if you were running around and took photos in several different locations on the same day. Provided there was at least a two-hour window between the times you took the photos at those different locations, you have a better chance of iPhoto sorting those locations into their own events.

Don't fret, however. As you'll soon discover, you can arrange and sort photos into any event you choose. Also, in Chapter 6 you'll learn that iPhoto has a powerful feature called Places, which sorts your photos based on the exact location where they were taken.

Imported Events

After you've imported your photos, they appear as events in the main body of iPhoto's window (Figure 4–2). For a refresher of importing photos, check out Chapter 2.

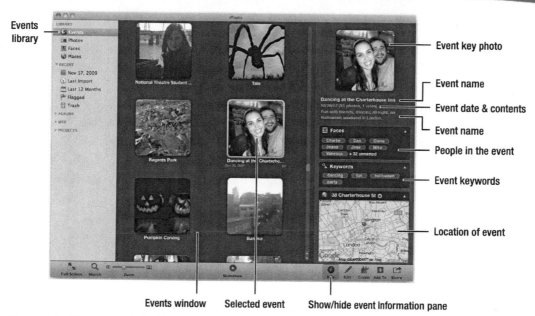

Events library

Event key photo

Event name

Event date & contents

Event name

People in the event

Event keywords

Location of event

Events window   Selected event   Show/hide event Information pane

Figure 4–2. *Viewing events in iPhoto*

In Figure 4–2, you can see what iPhoto looks like when you are viewing events. To view your events, make sure you have **Events** selected in iPhoto's source list. You'll notice that your events are arranged one after the other as a series of squares with rounded corners. If you move your mouse's cursor horizontally over an event, you'll see all the photos in that event in sequential order. Double-click an event to display all the photos it contains.

Event Information Pane

I talked in detail about the Information pane in Chapter 3, but I'll touch on it briefly here as to how it relates to events. To open the Information pane, click the **Info** button in the toolbar. In Figure 4–2, the event Information pane is displayed.

The Information pane shows the following information for a selected event:

- **Key photo:** The key photo is the photo that represents the event. It's a single photo from all the ones contained in the event. I'll talk more about key photos in a bit.

- **Event name:** Below the key photo you will find the name of the event. By default the event is named after the date the photos were taken on. You can change the name of the event just like you would change the name of a single photo. Click its name in the Information pane, and type in any name you want. You can also change the event's name by clicking its current name below its thumbnail in the events window.

■ **Event date and contents:** Below the event's name, you'll see the date or date range of the photos contained in the event. You'll also see how many items are contained in the event. In Figure 4–2, there are 91 photos and 1 video in the selected event.

■ **Faces:** When expanded, the Faces bar tells you who is in the photos contained in the event. In Figure 4–2 there are 7 recognized people in the photos and 32 unrecognized people. You'll learn all about the Faces feature in Chapter 5.

■ **Keywords:** This lists all the keywords of the photos contained in the event. You can add additional keywords by clicking in the **Keyword** field. Adding a keyword to an event adds that keyword to every photo in the event.

■ **Location:** The map at the bottom shows you the location the photos were taken in. I will talk all about iPhoto's location feature, Places, in Chapter 6.

Setting a Key Photo

As mentioned earlier, each event has a key photo that visually represents all the photos in that event. By default, an event's key photo is chosen by iPhoto, and it will always be the first photo in the event. However, you can change any event's key photo—and you probably should.

A good key photo lets you recognize an entire group of photos just by seeing that one image. For example, if you took your kids to the pumpkin patch, your first photo might have been of an ear of corn; however, a more representational photo of the event would probably be the one you took of that huge pumpkin.

To change an event's key photo, you have six (six!) options:

■ With events selected in the source list, run your mouse over any event so you are skimming through the event's photos. When you find a photo you like, stop skimming and press the spacebar on your keyboard. This sets the selected photo as the key photo.

■ With events selected in the source list, run your mouse over any event so you are skimming through the event's photos. When you find a photo you like, stop skimming and right-click. In the contextual menu that appears, select **Make Key Photo**.

■ Select an event so a yellow box highlights it. In the event Information pane, skim your mouse over the event so its photos are displayed one after another. Click the photo you want to set as the key photo.

- Double-click an event to view its contents. Scroll through the photos in the event, and when you find the one you want to make the key photo, right-click it and, in the contextual menu that appears, select **Make Key Photo**.

- Double-click an event to view its contents. Scroll through the photos in the event, and when you find the one you want to make the key photo, right-click it and, in the contextual menu that appears, select **Make Key Photo**.

- Double-click an event to view its contents. Scroll through the photos in the event, and when you find the one you want to make the key photo, select **Events ➤ Make Key Photo** from iPhoto's menu bar at the top of your screen.

Creating New Events

You aren't limited to only the events iPhoto has automatically created for you. iPhoto gives you the power to create new additional events based on three criteria: creating events using specific photos, creating events using flagged photos, and creating empty events.

Creating a New Event Using Specific Photos

Creating events using specific photos allows you to easily combine any photos, no matter where you took them or the length of time between taking them, into a single event. To create an event using specific photos (see Figure 4–3), follow these steps:

1. Select **Photos** in iPhoto's source list. The Photos list shows you every single photo in your Library regardless of what event or album it is located in.

2. Select the photos you want in your new event. To select a group of photos, click and drag your mouse over a selection of them. To select photos that are not near each other in the library, hold down the Command key on the keyboard, and click each desired photo so that a yellow box highlights them.

3. Choose **Events ➤ Create Event** from the menu bar. A warning box will show up that tells you a photo can appear in only one event at a time and that by moving these photos to a new event you will be removing them from the events they were located in. Click **Create**.

4. A new event is created in your events list. The new event is named based on the date of the first photo in the event, so you may need to scroll through your events list to see the new event if the first photo was taken well in the past.

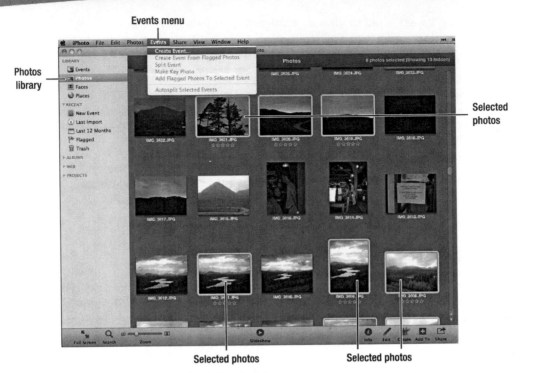

Figure 4–3. *Creating a new event using selected photos*

Creating a New Event Using Flagged Photos

You can quickly create a new event using the photos you have previously flagged. For a quick reminder on the benefits of flagging photos and how to flag them, see Chapter 3.

To create a new event using flagged photos, follow these steps:

1. Make sure you have flagged the photos you want in your new event.

2. Choose **Events ▶ Create Event From Flagged Photos** in the menu bar (Figure 4–4). A warning box will tell you a photo can appear in only one event at a time and that by moving these photos to a new event you will be removing them from the events they were located in. Click **Create**.

3. A new event is created in your events list. The new event is named based on the date of the first flagged photo in the event, so you may need to scroll through your events list to see the new event if the first photo was taken well in the past.

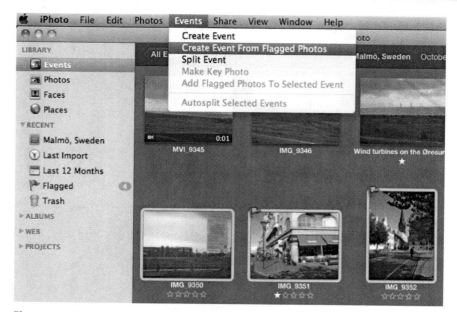

Figure 4–4. *Creating an event based on flagged photos*

Create an Empty Event

You can create an empty event and then fill it with photos of your choosing at a later time. To create an empty event, follow these steps:

1. Make sure you have selected events in the source list.

2. Make sure no events are selected in the main viewing window. Choose **Events ➤ Create Event** from the menu bar.

3. A placeholder event thumbnail appears in your events labeled **New Event**. As you can see in Figure 4–5, the event's key photo is actually just a thumbnail of a black-and-white palm tree and sunset.

4. You can then add photos to this empty event by simply dragging and dropping them into it.

Figure 4–5. *An empty event*

Merging Events

Merging events is a cool feature that allows you to combine two or more events into one. This is handy if you frequently visit and photograph the same location many times a year. For example, I have several events with pictures of Chicago. I can combine them into one event so I can see all of them in one place. Another reason you might merge events is to assemble all of your kid's birthday photos from their parties over the years into one event.

To merge two or more events, follow these steps:

1. Select Events in iPhoto's source list.

2. Select two or more events you want to merge. You can drag a box around close events to select them or hold down the Command key on the keyboard to select events that are farther away from each other.

3. Choose Events ➤ Merge Events from the menu bar, or right-click any of the selected events and choose Merge Events from the pop-up menu.

4. In the dialog that appears, you'll be warned that the photos from the selected events will be moved into one event. Click Merge.

You can also merge two events by simply dragging one event on top of another event (Figure 4–6). Doing so adds all the photos of the dragged event to the stationary event. The name and key photo of the stationary event is the one used for the merged photos. In Figure 4–6, the event highlighted in yellow is being dragged to the Bank of England event.

Figure 4–6. *Merging events by dragging and dropping one onto the other*

Splitting Events

Just as you can merge two events into one, you can split one event into two. This is really handy if you've been importing your photos using one day for the event autosplit settings and now want to divide that day's photos into more manageable chunks.

To split an event, follow these steps:

1. Select Events in iPhoto's source list.

2. Double-click the event you want to split so you can see the photos in that event.

3. Find and click the photo that you want to be the start of a new event. All photos that appear after this photo are added to the new event. If you want to split an event using nonadjacent photos from the event, hold down the Command key on the keyboard, and click the individual photos you want to split off from the main event.

4. Choose Events ➤ Split Event from iPhoto's menu bar.

In Figure 4–7 you can see the results of an event split. The Belfast event was split. All the photos before the split remain in the original event. Below that event is the newly split event, titled **untitled event**. You can double-click **untitled event** to rename it.

Figure 4–7. *The newly split event*

Events vs. Albums

At first glance it's a bit hard to tell the difference between an event and an album. They both are ways of organizing your iPhoto Library and can contain multiple photos. So, what are the differences?

- An individual photo can be contained in only one event, but the same photo can be placed in multiple albums.

- Photos in an event are arranged by their import sequence; you can't manually arrange them. With a photo album, you can arrange the photos in any order you want.

Albums are great because you can create an unlimited number of them to suit your needs. Think of an album in iPhoto as you would a traditional physical photo album. You can arrange and sort your photos how you like, add or remove photos without affecting their other locations in your iPhoto Library, and put the same photo in two or more places at once.

NOTE: No matter what, iPhoto does not keep two copies of your photos when you move them. If you have the same photo in three different albums, you still have only one copy of that photo in your iPhoto Library. When you place a photo in an album, you are effectively telling iPhoto to reference the photo from the main iPhoto Library.

Regular vs. Smart Albums

iPhoto lets you create two kinds of albums: regular and smart. Both types are similar in that they contain your photographs, but how you get photos into a regular album and a smart album differs greatly.

A regular album in iPhoto can contain any photo you manually add to it. Regular albums are great for grouping your favorite vacation shots or perhaps making a collection of photos that you want to burn to a CD and send to your grandma.

A smart album in iPhoto automatically groups any photos that match the criteria you set. For example, you might create a smart album to contain all the photos you have rated five stars. With a five-star smart album created, not only are you able to view all your five-star photos instantly, but also any photo you rate with five stars in the future automatically will be added to that smart album. As you'll see, you can create smart albums based on a wide assortment of criteria.

As you can see in Figure 4–8, all albums—both regular and smart—show up beneath the Albums header in iPhoto' source list. Depending on what you've created, you'll find the following here:

- **Folders:** Represented by a small blue folder icon, a folder can contain multiple albums. Folders allow you to group related albums, both regular and smart, together.

- **Smart albums:** A purple cog icon represents smart albums. They contain your photos based on predefined search criteria.

■ **Regular albums:** A regular album is represented by a blue photograph icon. Regular albums contain any photos you've manually dragged there.

Albums list

Album folder

Smart album

Selected album

Album

Contents of the
selected album

Figure 4–8. *Different kinds of albums in iPhoto's source list*

Creating Albums

iPhoto lets you create a regular album in a variety of ways. You can create empty albums, which you can then later populate at will, or you can create albums from currently selected events or photos or from a folder of photos on your Mac's hard drive.

Creating an Empty Album

To create an empty album, follow these steps:

1. From iPhoto's menu bar, choose **File ➤ New**; then hold down the Shift key and choose **Empty Album** from the submenu (Figure 4–9).

2. Your new album appears in the source list with the name **untitled album**. You can rename it to whatever you want by double-clicking the name.

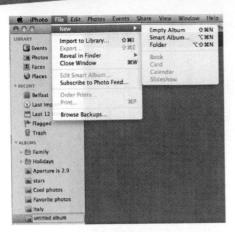

Figure 4–9. *Creating an empty album. Note the new untitled album item that appears in the source list.*

3. To add photos to the album, simply drag and drop them in one at a time, or select multiple photos and drag them in as a group.

4. When the selected photos are over the album, you'll be able to see how many will be added to the album via a red badge with a number in it displayed at the bottom of the dragged photo's thumbnail (Figure 4–10).

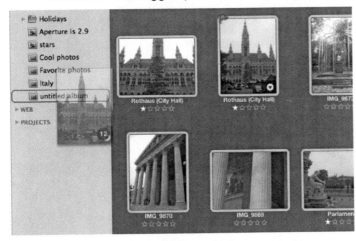

Figure 4–10. *Manually adding photos to an album*

NOTE: If you forget to hold down the Shift key while choosing File ➤ New, you will still create a new album, but it will be populated with every single photo in your library. You can go ahead and Select All (Command-A) and hit the Delete key to remove the photos to clear the album. The photos are still in your iPhoto Library.

Creating an Album from Selected Photos or Events

iPhoto allows you to select a group of photos or entire events and quickly create an album containing those photos. This is handy when you are browsing your photo library and see a collection of photos you'd like to group in their own album. It eliminates the need to create an empty album first and then drag the photos in later.

To create an album from selected photos, select the photo or photos you want to create an album from. You can then create the album using any of the following four ways:

- From iPhoto's menu bar, select File ➤ New Album. A new album containing the selected photos appears.

- Simply drag the selected photos to the iPhoto source list. A new album containing the selected photos appears.

- From iPhoto's toolbar at the bottom of the iPhoto window, click the Create button. It looks like a glue bottle and scissors. Select Album from the pop-up menu (Figure 4–11). A new album containing the selected photos appears.

Figure 4–11. *Creating a new album via the Create button*

- From iPhoto's toolbar at the bottom of the iPhoto window, click the Add To button. It looks like a + sign in a box. Select Album from the pop-up menu, and then select New Album from the expanded pop-up (Figure 4–12). A new album containing the selected photos appears.

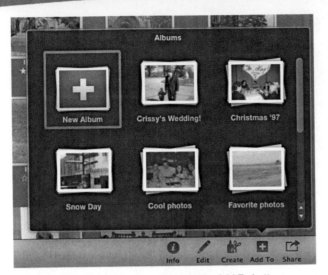

Figure 4–12. *Creating a new album via the Add To button*

Creating an Album from a Folder on Your Mac

If you have a folder full of photos on your Mac, you can quickly import them to your iPhoto Library and create an album at the same time. To do so, simply follow these steps:

1. Find the folder of photos on your Mac, and drag it to your iPhoto source list.

2. The import process begins, and when it finishes, you'll see all the photos contained in that folder in their own album.

3. The album is named after the original folder name. You can double-click it to rename it if you want.

Changing the Contents of Your Regular Albums

Once you've created a regular album, it will have the same contents in it until you choose to add or remove photos.

To add more photos to a regular album, follow these steps:

1. Select the photos you want to add from your iPhoto Library. The photos could be in an event or even another album.

2. Drag the selected photos to your desired album. Or, you can add more photos by selecting the photos, clicking the **Add To** button in the toolbar, and then selecting the album to which you want to add them.

To remove a photo from a regular album, follow these steps:

1. Select the album from iPhoto's source list.

2. Select the photo or photos you want to remove.

3. Tap the Delete key on your keyboard. Or, you can right-click one of the selected photos and choose **Remove from Album** from the contextual menu.

4. In the dialog box that asks whether you are sure you want to remove the selected photos, click **Remove Photos**.

iPhoto also lets you delete entire photo albums.

To delete an album, follow these steps:

1. Select the album from iPhoto's source list that you want to delete.

2. Hit the Delete key on your keyboard. Or, right-click the album in the source list, and choose Delete Album. Or, from iPhoto's menu bar, choose **Photos ➤ Delete Album**.

3. In the dialog box that asks whether you are sure you want to delete the album, click **Delete**.

NOTE: Remember, when you delete an album, you aren't deleting the photos it contains.

Creating Smart Albums

Now that you know how to create regular albums, you can see how useful they can be. They let you organize your photos in a way events do not—by putting the same photo in more than one location. However, as you can also see, regular albums involve a lot of manual work. To keep your albums updated, you must actively add or remove photos to them. Wouldn't it be great if there were a way to automatically add photos to albums? That's where smart albums come in.

Smart albums allow you to create albums containing photos based on certain parameters such as rating, EXIF information, text or description, date, keywords, and more. The best thing of all is that when any future photos that are imported to your iPhoto Library show up, they'll automatically be added to any smart albums they match the criteria for.

To create a smart album, follow these steps:

1. Choose File ➤ New ➤ Smart Album from iPhoto's menu bar, or click the **Create** button in the toolbar and hold down the **Option** key on your keyboard. In the pop-up menu, **Album** changes to **Smart Album**. Click it to create a new smart album, or right-click in the source list and choose **New Smart Album** in the pop-up menu. The dialog box shown in Figure 4–13 will appear.

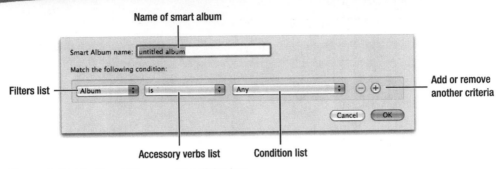

Figure 4–13. *The Smart Album creation dialog box*

2. From the Smart Album dialog box, enter the name of the smart album.

3. Choose a filter from the first drop-down menu. A filter is a specific criterion that must be matched for iPhoto to judge whether the particular item fits into one of your smart albums. A filter can be a keyword, the date the photo was taken, the photo's rating, or even EXIF information such as the camera's model or focal length.

4. Once you have selected a filter, choose a verb from the verb list. Common verbs in this list are **Is**, **Is not**, and **Contains**.

5. Finally, enter a requirement in the conditions list. This could be a star rating or a specific keyword.

6. To add additional criteria, click the + button, and choose additional criteria based on whatever you want. Next, select whether any or all of the multiple criteria must be met. When you are done, click OK, and the smart list appears under the Albums header in iPhoto's source list.

In Figure 4–14, I've set up a simple smart album named "Top stars" with the criteria that the My Rating setting "is greater than" three stars.

Smart Album name:	Top stars
Match the following condition:	
My Rating	is greater than	★★★☆☆	⊖ ⊕
		Cancel	OK

Figure 4–14. *A simple smart album with one condition*

As you can see in Figure 4–15, once I click OK, the smart album is created and can be found in my Albums list in iPhoto's source list. All the photos I have rated in my iPhoto Library as four stars or more show up in the album. If I were to reduce a photo's rating in that smart album from four to three stars, it would automatically be removed from the smart album because it does not meet the criteria anymore.

Figure 4–15. *A smart album based on four-star ratings or better*

Editing or Deleting Smart Albums

Just like with regular albums, iPhoto lets you edit and delete smart albums should you choose to do so.

To edit a smart album, follow these steps:

1. Select the smart album in iPhoto's source list.

2. Choose File ➤ Edit Smart Album from iPhoto's menu bar. Or, right-click the smart album, and choose Edit Smart Album from the pop-up menu.

3. In the Smart Album dialog box that appears, make changes to the existing criteria, or delete the criteria entirely. You can also add criteria by clicking the + button (see Figure 4–14).

To delete a smart album, follow these steps:

1. Select the smart album in iPhoto's source list.

2. Right-click the smart album, and choose **Delete Album** from the pop-up menu.

3. In the dialog box that appears, click **Delete** to confirm you want to delete the smart album.

Remember, deleting an album, regular or smart, does not delete the photos within that album. The photos are always contained in their event and any other albums you have not deleted.

Duplicating Albums

iPhoto lets you duplicate existing albums with just a few clicks. Why might you want to duplicate an album? Well, if it's a smart album, you might like your search criteria but want to tweak it a little yet still keep the original smart album. Duplicating it allows you to work from the original album without having to re-create it from scratch. The same goes for regular albums.

To duplicate an existing album, follow these steps:

1. Select the album in iPhoto's source list.

2. Choose **Photos ➤ Duplicate** from iPhoto's menu bar, or right-click the Album and choose **Duplicate** from the pop-up menu.

3. An exact duplicate of the album will be created with a 2 appended to its name.

Organizing Albums into Folders

I love creating both regular and smart albums, but sometimes things can get out of control when you have dozens of albums. When this happens, the things you've created to organize your photos become hard to organize. Luckily, iPhoto allows you to organize albums into folders. This allows you to group several albums. For example, all your travel albums can be grouped into one folder, or all your Christmas albums can be grouped into another.

Figure 4–16 shows you what your albums look like in iPhoto's source list before and after you group them into folders.

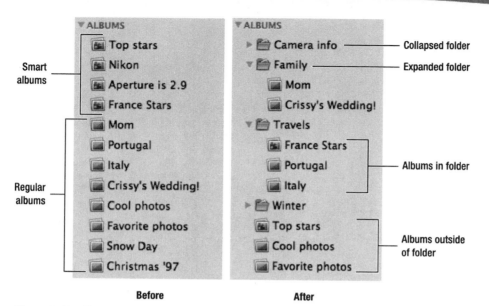

Figure 4–16. *Albums not in any folders (before) and in folders (after)*

The "before" picture in Figure 4–16 shows you how albums are arranged in iPhoto without any folders. The smart albums (purple) always come first, followed by the regular albums (blue).

In the "after" version in Figure 4–16, you can see what happens when you create folders. The folders always appear at the top of the albums list and contain whatever smart or regular albums you've dragged into them. Albums within a folder are indented. Any albums that are not sorted into folders show up after the last folder—smart coming before regular. As you can see, folders can contain both smart and regular albums.

To create a folder and fill it with albums, follow these steps:

1. Choose File ➤ New Folder from iPhoto's menu bar, or right-click anywhere in iPhoto's source list and choose New Folder from the pop-up menu.

2. A new untitled folder appears under the Albums heading. Double-click it to rename it.

3. To add an album to the folder, simply click any album, and drag it onto the folder.

> **TIP:** Clicking a folder displays all the photos in every album in that folder.

To remove an album from a folder, do this:

- Simply drag the album out of the folder and back into the source list or another folder.

To delete a folder, follow these steps:

1. Select the folder, and hit the Delete key on your keyboard. Or, right-click the folder, and choose **Delete Folder** from the pop-up menu.

2. A dialog box appears warning you that deleting a folder also deletes the albums in the folder. Click **Delete** to delete the folders and albums.

3. To delete only the folder and not the albums it contains, remove the albums from the folder first. If you delete a folder with no albums, it is removed instantly, and you will not see the Delete Folder confirmation box.

Arranging Your Albums

By now you understand you can sort your photos into albums and you can sort those albums into folders. You also understand the default arrangements of albums and folders: folders appear first, followed by smart albums and then regular albums.

However, you can drag folders and albums up or down the list so they appear in the order you want them. To drag a folder or album up or down the list, just click and hold it and then move it to the desired location.

If you don't feel like sorting all your albums but want to view them in alphabetical order, you can click anywhere in the Albums header in iPhoto's source list, right-click, and then choose **Sort Albums** from the pop-up menu (Figure 4–17). iPhoto instantly organizes all your folders and albums alphabetically.

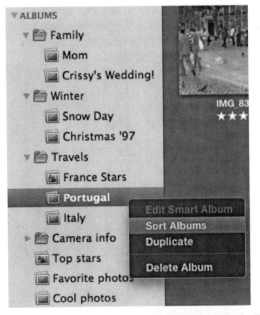

Figure 4–17. *Sorting albums and folders alphabetically*

Viewing Your Photos

Now you understand the ways events and albums help you organize your photos. Let's talk briefly about actually viewing your photos. In Figure 4–18, I've selected an album containing some of my favorite photos. Inside that album my photos are presented as thumbnails. At the bottom of the screen in iPhoto's toolbar, you will see the Zoom slider. Adjusting this slider increases and decreases the size of the thumbnails, which lets you see fewer or more of your photos at one time.

Figure 4–18. *Viewing photos in an album*

As you can see in Figure 4–19, I have moved the Zoom slider to the right, which increases the size of a photo's thumbnail. This allows me to see larger photos but fewer of all of the photos in the album at the same time.

TIP: If a photo in your album or event is rotated the wrong way—for example, it's horizontal when it should be vertical—you can quickly rotate it by right-clicking the photo and then selecting the **Rotate** button from the pop-up menu.

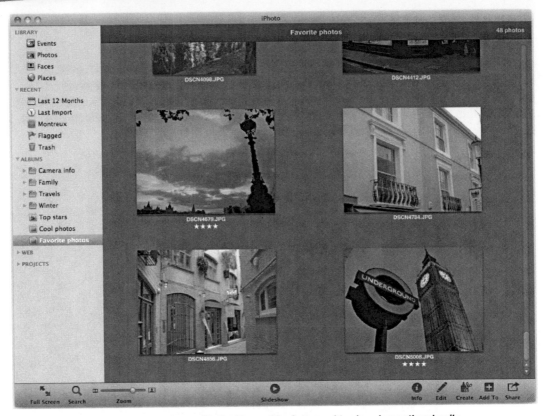

Figure 4–19. *Viewing the same album with the Zoom slider increased to show larger thumbnails*

To quickly view an individual photo, I can double-click it or select it and then press the spacebar on my keyboard. When I do, the photo springs forward to cover all the other photos (Figure 4–20).

Figure 4-20. *Viewing a photo*

You'll note that the toolbar at the bottom of iPhoto's window now shows a film roll. This film roll contains all the photos in the selected album or event. When you move your mouse over the film roll, it enlarges on your screen to make it easier to see the photo thumbnails (Figure 4–21).

Figure 4–21. *Skimming through the film roll*

Scroll through the film roll until you find a photo you want to view; then click it, and it appears in iPhoto's window.

Sorting Photos and Events

iPhoto allows you to sort the display order for your photos and events. By default, iPhoto shows you your events or your photos in albums and events from oldest to newest. Using the **View** menu in iPhoto can change this.

To sort events, follow these steps:

1. Select **Events** in iPhoto's source list, and then choose **View ➤ Sort Events**.

2. From the submenu, you can choose to sort events:

   ■ **By Date:** Arranges events by the date on which they were taken, from oldest to newest. You can reverse the order by choosing **View ➤ Sort Events** and then choosing Ascending or Descending.

   ■ **By Title:** Arranges events alphabetically by their titles.

   ■ **Manually:** Lets you drag events into any order you want.

To sort photos in events or albums, follow these steps:

1. Select the album or event containing the content you want to sort, and then choose **View ➤ Sort Photos**.

2. From the submenu, you can choose to sort photos:

    ■ **By Date:** Arranges photos by the date on which they were taken, from oldest to newest. You can reverse the order by choosing **View ➤ Sort Photos** and then choosing Ascending or Descending.

    ■ **By Title:** Arranges photos alphabetically by their titles.

    ■ **Manually:** Lets you drag photos into any order you want. This option is not available for photos inside events or smart albums.

    ■ **By Rating:** Sorts photos from lowest to highest rating. You can reverse the order by choosing **View ➤ Sort Photos** and then choosing Ascending or Descending.

Summary

As you can see, iPhoto has no shortage of great ways to organize and navigate your photos. With events, you can keep your photo library organized with zero effort on your part if you so choose. For those of you who need more control, you can edit and create new events and also sort your photos into two kinds of albums—regular and smart.

There are, however, two more ways iPhoto allows you to organize your photo library. The first is called Faces, which I talk about next chapter. Then in Chapter 6 I introduce you to the last organizational technique, called Places.

Chapter 5

Organizing Your Photos: Faces

Faces is one of those features of iPhoto that makes you take a step back and go "Wow!" With Faces, iPhoto uses facial recognition technology built into the software to identify and group individuals into collections of photos. With Faces, you can easily see all pictures of your child, spouse, or a particular friend in a single location—the Faces corkboard.

Creating Faces Collections

To get started with Faces, select Faces in iPhoto's source list. By default, iPhoto will have scanned the photos in your iPhoto Library already to pick out and identify faces of people who appear in your photographs.

When you select Faces for the first time, you'll be taken to the Find Faces screen, as shown in Figure 5–1.

Figure 5–1. *Selecting faces in iPhoto*

The Find Faces screen displays thumbnails of people iPhoto thinks could be important to you. It's then up to you to name a person in the thumbnail or reject them. Naming a Face adds that face to the Faces corkboard.

To name a face, follow these steps:

1. Click **unnamed** in the naming field below the face.

2. Enter the name of the person in the photo. You can enter just their first name, first and last names, or even a nickname. As you begin entering a person's name, iPhoto displays the names of people who matched the text you entered so far from your Address Book, already-added faces, or Facebook friends (if you've signed into your Facebook account in iPhoto). I talk about Facebook integration in Chapter 9.

    You can click any of the selected results from the name pop-up menu to apply that name to the face, or you can continue entering a different name. One you have entered a name, press the Return key on your keyboard.

3. You can continue to name the unnamed faces displayed to you. Note that in Figure 5–1 three faces are displayed at a time. Depending on your screen size, iPhoto may show you more or fewer face suggestions at a time.

Sometimes you might not want to name a face that iPhoto has detected. Perhaps it's just a random person in a crowd or someone you don't like very much (like that pesky boss). iPhoto allows you to ignore these faces.

To ignore a face, follow these steps:

1. Move your mouse over the face's thumbnail.

2. Click the white *x* inside the black circle at the upper-left corner of the thumbnail. The face thumbnail fades, signifying that iPhoto knows to ignore it in the future.

3. If you have mistakenly told iPhoto to ignore a face you want to track, move your mouse over the thumbnail again, and click the *x* a second time.

Once you have completed naming or ignoring the faces on the screen, you can click the **Show More Faces** button to see more faces. iPhoto displays another series of faces that you can choose to name or ignore.

When you are done naming faces, click the **Continue to Faces** button. This takes you to the Faces corkboard where your selected faces are displayed.

> **TIP:** In case you were wondering, Faces can actually recognize the faces of your pets. It's not always 100 percent accurate, but my cat was identified just fine in more than 20 photos. Faces will also register statues, paintings, or photographs of people in the photograph (say, on the wall behind the person being photographed) as "faces" too.

The Faces Corkboard

As you can see in Figure 5–2, the Faces corkboard displays collections of photos that your family and friends appear in. After the first time you name people in Faces, you'll automatically be taken to the Faces corkboard when you select **Faces** from iPhoto's source list.

A thumbnail photograph that looks like an old Polaroid picture represents each Faces collection. Below a Faces collection is the name of the person written in Felt Marker font. When you are on the corkboard, double-click any Faces collection to see all the photos that iPhoto has recognized that person in.

You can also change the name of the person at any time by double-clicking their existing name and entering a new one.

As you skim your mouse across each Faces collection, you'll see a close-up, or headshot, of the individual's face in every photo they appear in that iPhoto has recognized. You can use any headshot as the key photo for that particular Faces collection. The key photo is the image that appears in the Polaroid-type border.

To set a key photo for a face, follow these steps:

1. Skim your cursor left to right over the Faces collection.

2. When you find the photo that you want to represent the person in the collection, press the spacebar on your keyboard, or right-click and choose **Make Key Photo** from the pop-up menu.

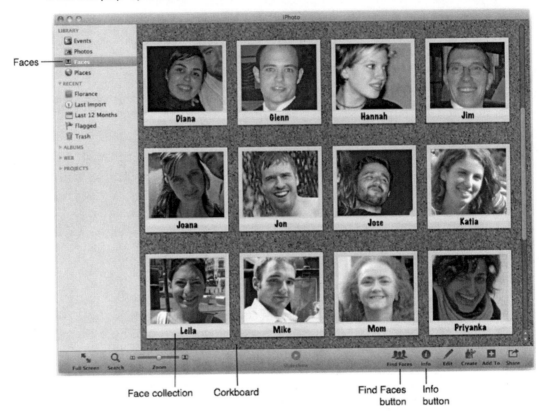

Figure 5–2. *Faces groups your photos by the people in them using facial recognition.*

The Faces Information Pane

As with events and individual photos, clicking the **Info** button in the toolbar while on the Faces corkboard provides more information about the selected Faces collection. From top to bottom, the Faces Information pane (Figure 5–3) displays the following:

- **Key photo:** This is the thumbnail that represents the person for the Faces collection. You can change the key photo in the Information pane by running your mouse across it and clicking when you see the photo you'd like to set. Changing the key photo here also changes the key photo on the corkboard.

- **Add a full name:** In this field, you can enter the full name of the person in the Faces collection. This is handy when you might have the collection name displayed on the corkboard as "Mom" or a nickname like "Kaboom" but you want to enter the person's actual name to use for searches.

- **Add an email address:** In this field, you can enter the e-mail address for the person in the Faces collection. At first this feature might seem rather random, but it actually comes in handy when you start using the integrated Facebook features of iPhoto. If you have an e-mail address associated with a Face, iPhoto uses that information to work with Facebook in accurately identifying Facebook friends in your photos when you upload them. I talk more about iPhoto's Faces feature as it relates to Facebook later in this chapter. Then in Chapter 9, I discuss the additional Facebook integration that iPhoto '11 offers.

Figure 5–3. *The Faces corkboard with the Info pane displayed*

- **Date range:** This tells you the range of dates the photos in the collection were taken. If you have baby photos of your grandpa, this date range could be decades.

- **Number of photos:** This is the number of photos of the person in the Faces collection.

- **Unconfirmed matches:** This tells you the number of photos iPhoto thinks the selected individual might be in. Clicking the arrow will take you to the photo confirmation screen.

■ **Location:** This area displays a map of the various locations of the photos the person appears in.

Inside a Faces Collection

To view the photos inside a select Faces collection, double-click the Faces thumbnail. As you can see in Figure 5–4, all the photos that iPhoto has recognized as a particular individual appear.

Figure 5–4. *A Faces collection in Faces view*

By default, you'll see only the headshots of the selected person. To view the entire photo, click the **Photos/Faces** slider in the upper-right corner. All the headshots of the person will change to full photographs, as shown in Figure 5–5.

Figure 5–5. *A Faces collection in Photos view*

A Faces collection acts just like a smart album for the most part, with the exception that the Faces "album" only contains photographs of the same person and cannot have any other criteria applied to it.

Confirming or Rejecting Suggested Matches in a Faces Collection

Every time you import photos to your library, iPhoto automatically scans them to detect any known or unknown faces. When iPhoto thinks it may have a match for an existing person in your Faces collection, it displays a notification in two locations:

- When a face is selected on the corkboard and the Information pane is open, you'll see an "Unconfirmed matches" note (Figure 5–3). Click the arrow to enter the Faces confirmation screen (Figure 5–6).

- When you double-click to view the photos in a Face collection, you'll see an "Additional Photos" note in the blue bar at the bottom of the screen. In Figure 5–5 iPhoto thinks Diana may be in 38 additional photographs. Click the **Confirm Additional Faces** button to enter the Faces confirmation screen (Figure 5–6).

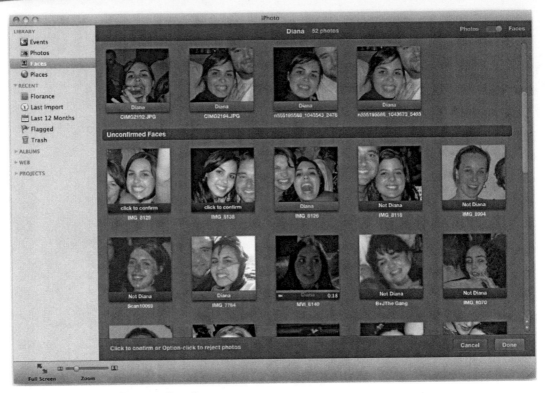

Figure 5–6. *Additional Faces confirmation screen*

On the Faces confirmation screen you'll see the existing photos with your selected person, followed by photos that iPhoto thinks the person may be in. These unconfirmed Faces photos all have a black **Click to Confirm** bar running along the bottom.

- To confirm that the person in the photo *matches* the person in the Faces collection, click an unconfirmed photo once. The black **Click to Confirm** bar changes to green, and the person's name appears in it.

- If the person in the unconfirmed photo *is not a match* for the person in the Faces collection, click the photo twice so the black bar changes from black to green and finally to red. The red bar will read "Not [name]." You can also hold down the Option key on your keyboard and click a photo once to confirm it is not a match.

You can confirm or deny multiple matches at the same time by selecting a group of unconfirmed photos; just drag the mouse around them, and then simply click any of the selected photos once to confirm they are a match or twice to confirm they are not a match. Click the **Done** button to finalize your selection. If you've made a mistake, you can always go back and click the green confirmed bar for any photo to tell iPhoto that photo is not a match. The photo will be removed from that Faces collection.

Confirmed faces become part of that person's Faces collection. Confirming faces increases iPhoto's accuracy at predicting who appears in one of your photos, so it's a good idea to check frequently to see whether iPhoto has any faces suggestions for you.

Rescanning Your Photo Library for Faces

If you know the person in your selected Faces collection is in other photographs despite them not showing up in the Additional Faces confirmation screen, you can tell iPhoto to rescan all the photos in your library.

iPhoto will rescan your library with less stringent criteria than in the original scan. This can result in more false positives for the selected individual, however.

To rescan your library for faces, follow these steps:

1. Choose Photo ➤ Detect Missing Faces from iPhoto's menu bar. During a rescan, iPhoto uses less strict criteria for determining a face, which could result in more matches.

2. You can then return to your Faces collection and see whether iPhoto has found any other unconfirmed matches for your Faces collections, or you can click the Find Faces button in the toolbar, which takes you to the Find Faces screen (Figure 5–1), and see whether iPhoto has picked up any new faces in your photo library.

Naming Faces and Adding Missing Faces Manually

Sometimes iPhoto won't recognize that certain people who already have a Faces collection are in other photos. This can be because of the angle of the person's face in the photo, or perhaps there is a large age gap in the person from one photo to the next (like if you have a picture of your grandma when she was ten and another when she was eighty).

Other times iPhoto may not even detect a face in a photo. This is primarily because of the angle of the face in the photo or the quality of the image. In either case, you can manually add a person to an existing Faces collection or tell iPhoto that it is not detecting a face in a photograph.

If iPhoto doesn't recognize a person you know is in another photograph, follow these steps:

1. Navigate to the photo that contains the person in your iPhoto Library.

2. Make sure the Information pane is open by clicking the Info button in the toolbar.

3. If iPhoto has detected their face already, click the unnamed pop-up menu under their face, and enter the name of the person. Doing this tells iPhoto it is indeed the same person as the one in the Faces collection, and therefore iPhoto might now return more unconfirmed results.

TIP: You can also use the previous steps to create Faces collections when viewing a photo instead of using the Find Faces feature. This means you can jump right in to naming your favorite people instead of relying on iPhoto to pick out their faces.

If iPhoto doesn't detect a face in a photograph, follow these steps:

1. Navigate to the photo that contains the person in your iPhoto Library.

2. Make sure the Information pane is open by clicking the **Info** button in the toolbar.

3. Click the **Add a Face** button under the Faces header in the Information pane (Figure 5–7).

4. A new **Face** field appears over the selected photo. You can drag and resize this new face field to the correct location—that location being the unrecognized face.

5. Once the **New Face** field is in position, click the **click to name** pop-up menu, and add the name of the person. If it is of an existing person in a Faces collection, the photo is added to that collection. If it is of a new person, a new Face collection is added to the Faces corkboard.

Figure 5–7. *Adding a face manually*

TIP: When adding Faces manually, it is a good idea to find a photo of the person in profile, as well as head-on, and name both. Naming both profile shots of people and head-on shots gives iPhoto a better chance of finding more photos of them no matter what their orientation in the photograph.

Removing People

iPhoto allows you to remove a Faces collection from your corkboard should you so choose. This is especially handy if you want to stop tracking which photos a certain person appears in—say, your ex—or if you've just decided you don't need to create a Faces collection for every single person in your iPhoto Library, like the hotdog vendor on 53rd Street.

To remove a Faces collection from your corkboard, follow these steps:

1. Click Faces in iPhoto's source list.

2. Select the Faces collection you want to remove so it is highlighted in a blue border.

3. Hold the Command key on your keyboard, and then press the Delete key.

4. In the dialog that appears, click the **Delete** button. The person's collection is removed from the corkboard, and their name is removed from any photo they appear in. The photos in which they appear still remain in your iPhoto Library.

Using Faces with Facebook

It seems everyone these days is using Facebook, and one of the big features of Facebook is photo sharing. With iPhoto '11, Apple has made it easy for you to post photos from your iPhoto Library directly to your Facebook wall. I talk about Facebook sharing, including setting up iPhoto for use with your Facebook account, in Chapter 9. For now, though, let's briefly talk about how Faces works with Facebook.

Facebook lets you add names to people in photographs that you post on the site—just like how iPhoto lets you add names to people in photographs in your iPhoto Library. When you add a name to a person in a Facebook photo, Facebook calls it *tagging*. Naming Faces in iPhoto works hand in hand with tagging people in Facebook photos.

Specifically, when you upload a photo to Facebook through iPhoto's sharing features (see Chapter 9), any names you have applied to people in your photos are cross-checked with your Facebook friends. This is done by checking the e-mail address associated with your Faces collections. If the e-mail address assigned to a Faces collection matches the e-mail address a friend uses to log into their Facebook account, Facebook knows to apply a tag of that person to the photo once it is posted (Figure 5–8).

Abbey Named in iPhoto   Abbey Tagged on Facebook

Figure 5–8. *The image of Abbey on the left was named using Faces. When that image was uploaded to Facebook (right), Facebook knew to tag her in it automatically even though she uses her full name—Abigail—on Facebook.*

So, if you've named a photo of a person in iPhoto, there's no need to tag that person on Facebook.com if you've uploaded it through iPhoto's built-in Facebook sharing feature. Pretty cool, huh?

Summary

The Faces feature, like events, albums, and smart albums, is just another excellent and fun way iPhoto lets you easily sort, navigate, and organize your photos into manageable collections. It also shows you the power of iPhoto. I mean, whoever thought that our computers would be able to pick out and identify our friends and family in our photographs with very little effort on our part?

Now that you're acquainted with Faces, there's still one last cool way iPhoto lets you organize your photographs, and that's by location. In the next chapter, you'll learn about Places, which lets you travel the globe as you relive your photo memories.

Chapter 6

Organizing Your Photos: Places

Places is probably my favorite feature of iPhoto '11. If you're a travel buff like me, you can see just how cool a feature it is. With Places, you can easily track all the locations where you took your photos on a large, interactive Google map. Simply select any pin on the map to view all the photos you took in that location and relive your travels all over again.

In this chapter, you'll learn how to navigate the Places map, how to manually add or remove Places locations, and how to easily create smart albums from within Places. But first, let's talk about how Places can automatically "know" where you photos were taken—and that's by using location data.

What Is Location Data?

Location data consists of bits of information encoded into the photographs you take that helps your camera or photo software accurately pinpoint the location of the photo you have taken. When you take a picture, there are two ways your photos can be automatically tagged with location data. The first is by GPS, and the second is by using a known Wi-Fi location.

Depending on the camera being used, you may have one of these technologies built into the hardware. For example, most smartphones, like the iPhone, have built-in GPS chips that will tag your photos with their location. Some newer cameras, like the Nikon Coolpix P6000 or the Panasonic DMC-ZS7 series, also have GPS chips built in.

The Global Positioning System (GPS) is a way for the device you are using, such as a phone or computer, to know where it is at any given moment. It does this via a built-in chip that receives coded transmissions from a number of satellites high above the earth. The built-in chip knows where each satellite should be at any particular point in time and can use that data to interpret and calculate its own location with great accuracy. In a camera with GPS capabilities, these coordinates are encoded in the EXIF information (see Chapter 3) of each photograph you take. That EXIF information is then extracted by iPhoto, which uses it to display your photos' locations on a map.

A second way the device you are using to take pictures can encode location data is by using Wi-Fi location services. If your camera or smartphone has a Wi-Fi chip built into it, it may—depending on the device—be able to encode approximate location data into your photo's EXIF information that can then be used later to "guesstimate" the approximate location your photos were taken. It does this by using known Wi-Fi hotspots, and their known locations, to narrow in on the location your photo was taken. Wi-Fi location services aren't as accurate as dedicated built-in GPS chips, but they do at least put your photos in the right ballpark. Keep in mind, however, that Wi-Fi location services are essentially worthless when your device is out of the range of known Wi-Fi hotspots.

> **TIP:** Love your camera but wish it had location data services built-in? There's no need to buy an expensive new one. Just pick up a Wi-Fi-enabled SD card for your camera like the Eye-Fi Geo X2. It's simply an SD memory card for you camera, like the one you are using now, but it has Wi-Fi built into the memory card. Any photos you take on the card will have the Wi-Fi location data encoded on them, which will then be used to show you their Places location when you import them into iPhoto! Pretty cool, huh? A 4GB Eye-Fi Geo X2 card costs $69 at the time of this writing and is available at www.eye.fi.

However, if you have an older camera without location data capabilities, you aren't barred from using Places in iPhoto. iPhoto allows you to manually enter location for your photos so they'll appear on the Places map. I'll show you how to do that later in the chapter.

Setting Up iPhoto to Use Your Location Data

Just because your camera tags your photos with location data doesn't mean iPhoto automatically displays your photos on the Places map. You must first make sure you allow iPhoto to access the location data for your photographs. To do so, follow these steps:

1. Choose iPhoto ➤ Preferences from iPhoto's menu bar.

2. Click the Advanced tab (Figure 6–1).

3. Make sure Look up Places is set to Automatically. If it is set to Never, iPhoto will not read the location data from the EXIF information in your photos.

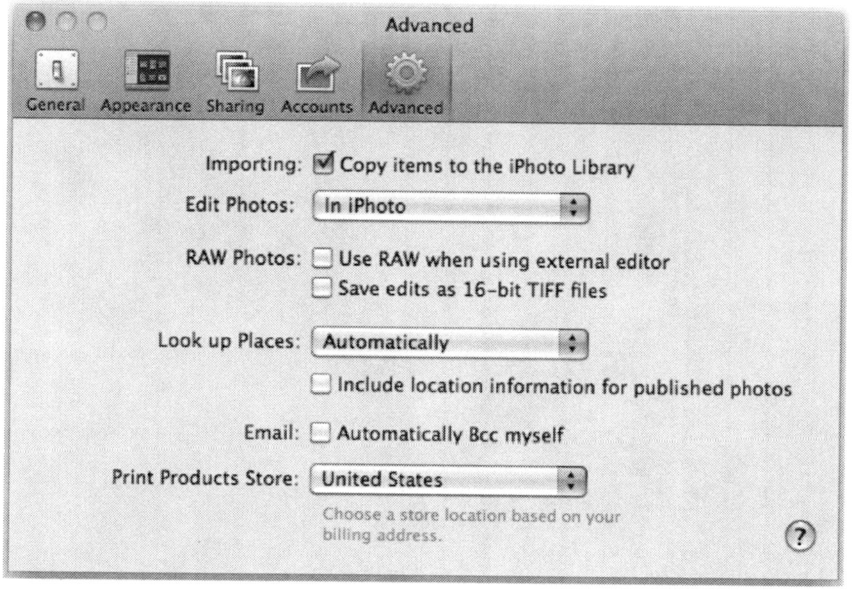

Figure 6–1. *iPhoto's location preferences*

You can also select the **Include location information for published photos** check box if you want your photo's location published when you share the photo on MobileMe, Facebook, or Flickr. I'll talk about iPhoto's photo-sharing features in Chapter 10.

It is also important to note that iPhoto will not display your photo's location information without an Internet connection. When iPhoto reads your photos' location data, it fetches information from the Internet in order to display their correct locations on the Places map. Without an Internet connection, the Places map will not appear in iPhoto.

So if you are using iPhoto somewhere without an Internet connection, you will not be able to view your photos using Places. You will, however, be able to view all your photos with a Places location by choosing **Places** from iPhoto's source list and then clicking the **Show Photos** button at the bottom of the screen.

The Places Map

When you select Places from iPhoto's source list, you are presented with a Google map that shows a series of red pins on it (see Figure 6–2). Each red pin represents a location where your photos were taken.

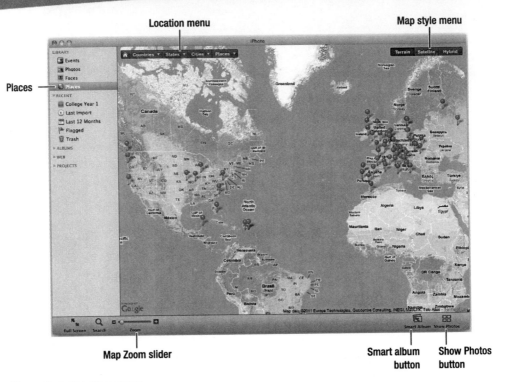

Figure 6-2. *The Places map*

While viewing the Places map, you should be aware of some elements. I go into all these features throughout the chapter, but let's briefly look at them now:

- **Location menu:** Located at the top left of the map, this menu allows you to jump to specific regions on your map including country, state, city, or places.

- **Maps style menu:** This menu is used to switch between three map views: Terrain, Satellite, and Hybrid.

- **Map Zoom slider:** This slider, located below the map, works for the map just the same as it does for zooming in on your photos. Move the slider left or right to zoom out or zoom in on the map.

- **Smart Album button:** This button allows you to create a smart album of the photos from the currently showing pins on the map.

- **Show Photos button:** When clicked, this button displays a contact sheet of all the photos of the current pins in view.

Before you move on, it should be noted that the map in Places view is read-only. That means you cannot edit or change locations of photos by dragging the pins around. Everything on the Places map is stationary and fixed. However, the mini-map in the Information pane of a photo or event is where you edit locations and make changes to your photos. I'll talk about this mini-map in detail later in the chapter.

Navigating the Places Map Manually

iPhoto allows you to manually interact with the Places map in two primary ways: by using the Zoom slider or by using your trackpad or mouse. Use the Zoom slider by moving its tiny ball left or right; as you do so, the map zooms in or out. You can also use the scroll wheel on your mouse to zoom in or out on the map. If you have an Apple Magic Mouse, simply slide your finger up and down on the mouse to zoom in and out.

As you zoom into a location, you may notice more pins appear. This signifies different locations for photos in a more defined area. For example, in Figure 6–2 there are three pins representing photo locations in England, but when I zoom into England in Figure 6–3, eight pins appear. iPhoto limits the number of pins you see when viewing the map in its entirety in order to not clutter the map with thousands of pins. The more you zoom into one location, the more pins you are likely to see, provided you have photos in multiple locations.

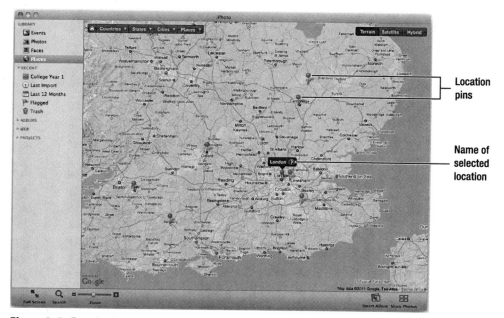

Figure 6–3. *Zooming in on the map and selecting a location*

Once you have zoomed in on a location, you can click and hold your mouse to drag the map around. When you click and hold the mouse button on the map, your cursor icon turns into a hand.

Navigating the Places Map Using the Location Menu

In addition to using the zoom slider in iPhoto's toolbar, or your mouse or trackpad to navigate the map, you can also use the location menu to instantly jump to a specific location on the map. The location menu is the semi-transparent bar at the top left of the map. It consists of a home button, followed by buttons for countries, states, cities, and places.

In Figure 6–4, you can see I have selected the **Countries** button from the location menu. Any countries where I have taken photos are listed in the drop-down menu. Countries where no photos were taken are not listed. I can click any country in the list to be taken to its location on the map.

Figure 6–4. *Navigating the map with the location menu*

When selecting a location from the location menu—a country, for instance—you will not see the entire country on the screen; you will see a zoomed-in portion of the country where you have taken photos. For example, in Figure 6–5, I have chosen Ireland after clicking the Countries button. iPhoto has zoomed into only the locations in Ireland where I have taken photos.

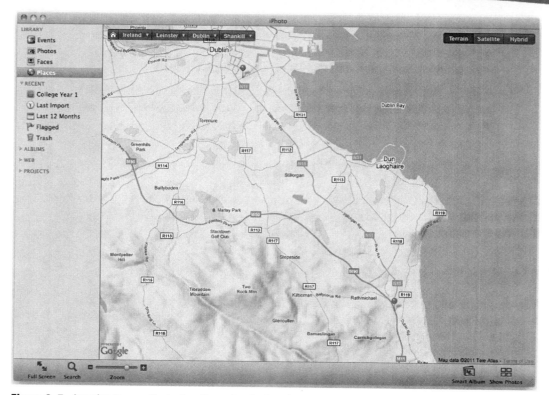

Figure 6–5. *Jumping to a particular location using the location menu*

In Figure 6–5 you'll also note that the location menu is dynamic. That is, since I have selected Ireland as my country, in the State menu I'll only see states or provinces listed where I have taken photos in Ireland, and in the Cities menu I will only see the Irish cities listed where I took photos in Ireland. The same goes for the Places menu.

To quickly zoom out to view all your pins on the map, click the home button in the location menu. That's the button that looks like a house icon. One last thing about the location menu before I move on: the last button is called Places. The Places button shows you a menu of all the individual locations of your photos, including specific addresses, such as your home address, or points of interest, such as the Eiffel Tower.

Switching Between Map Views

iPhoto gives you three options of how to view the map that your photos are presented on in Places. You can switch between these map views using the map style menu in the upper-right corner of the map.

- **Terrain:** This view shows you the topography of given map. This view lets you see relief maps of an area's terrain. The Terrain view also overlays roads, borders, and labels.

- **Satellite:** This view shows you the world using satellite imagery. It's perhaps the coolest map view because you can zoom in on streets and see little blips of people walking the day the satellite imagery (not your photos) was taken. No labels appear in Satellite view.

- **Hybrid:** This view combines Terrain and Satellite views. You see the map in satellite imagery, but it has labels, roads, and borders overlaid on it.

Viewing Your Photos in Places

Places isn't just about viewing pins on a map, of course. Places allows you to easily see all the photos you have taken in a given area. It does this in one of two ways: pins and the Show Photos button.

Viewing Photos by Pin

You can click any pin to see all the photos taken at that location. When you click a pin, a black label with the name of the location appears over the pin with an arrow (>) icon on it (Figure 6–6). If you are zoomed out relatively far on the map, the pin may contain different locations in it.

Figure 6–6. *Click a label's arrow (>) icon to view all the photos taken in that location.*

Note that if you click the red head of a pin, it turns yellow. This keeps that pin's label up while you navigate your mouse to other locations on the map. Click the arrow (>) icon on the pin's label to be taken to the contact-sheet view of all the photos at that pin's location (Figure 6–7).

Figure 6–7. *The photo's contained in the London pin in Figure 6–6*

In Figure 6–7, you can see all the photos that are contained in the London pin. Inside that pin are actually 26 locations, which you would see individual pins for if you zoomed in enough. However, at the location I chose to display the London pin's photos, you can see all the photos for those 26 locations in London. Click the Map button in the upper-left corner to return to the map view.

Viewing Photos Using the Show Photos Button

A second way to view photos on the map is by clicking the Show Photos button below the map in iPhoto's toolbar (Figure 6–8).

Figure 6–8. *The Show Photos button displays the photos for all the pins in view on the map.*

The Show Photos button works a little differently when displaying photos than selecting a pin does. If you click the Show Photos button, every photo for every pin viewable on the map is displayed in a window like the one in Figure 6–7. This is handy when you want to view photos from multiple locations that cannot be combined into one pin by zooming out on the map.

Places Mini-Maps in the Information Pane

Don't worry if you don't have a camera with location data capabilities. iPhoto lets you manually add location data to your photos quickly and easily. Additionally, iPhoto lets you change the location of a photograph that is already assigned a specific place.

You already explored the Information pane in detail in Chapter 3. It's the information window you access by clicking the Info button in the iPhoto toolbar. Inside every Information pane for any selected event, photo, or album, you'll see a Places header. When you expand the Places header, you'll see a mini-map (Figure 6–9) that shows the location of the selected photo or the locations of all the photos in a selected event.

Figure 6–9. *The mini-map shows you Places information in the Information pane.*

Just like on the large Places map, you can switch between Terrain, Satellite, and Hybrid views of the mini-maps in the Information pane, zoom in or out of the map, or click the center button—the one that looks like crosshairs—to center the pins on the map.

Manually Adding Locations to Photos

The mini-map is also where you can manually add a location to a photo. To do this, select a photo in your library that does not have a location assigned to it. You'll see the mini-map in the Information pane is blank (Figure 6–10).

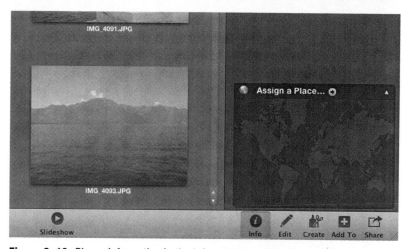

Figure 6–10. *Places information in the Information pane with no location assigned to the selected photo*

The photograph of the lake in Figure 6–10 is of Lake Geneva in Switzerland. If I want to add Lake Geneva as its location, I can simply do the following:

1. Click **Assign a Place** in the Places header in the Information pane.

2. Start typing a name, in this case, "Lake Geneva." As I begin to type "Lake Gene," iPhoto automatically cross-checks to see whether any other photos in my library have matching locations. iPhoto also displays major locations around the world, such as cities, and points of interest, such as the Eiffel Tower, as location suggestions (Figure 6–11).

   iPhoto also searches Google to see whether what you are typing matches any points of interest. You can also enter the exact address of a location if you know it or even the exact coordinates of a location. Just be sure to enter latitude before longitude.

Figure 6–11. *iPhoto automatically suggests Place locations as you type.*

3. To enter the location of the photo, click any of the location suggestions in the drop-down menu or simply finish typing the name of the desired location. iPhoto displays a map with a pin representing the photo's location (Figure 6–12).

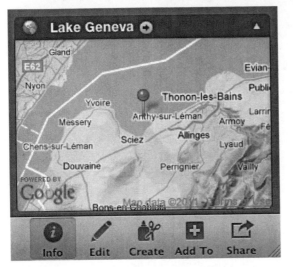

Figure 6–12. *The resulting map with location pin*

> **NOTE:** If adding locations to your photo's seem tedious, you can make it easier by selecting multiple photos you know were taken in the same location—be it a particular house or just the same city—and then using the same steps outlines earlier to assign a new place to all the photos selected at one time. You can also assign a location to an event. When you do, all the photos in the event are tagged with that location. You can then change individual photo's locations inside that event without affecting the other photos.

Manually Moving a Pin

Sometimes when you enter a fairly wide-ranging area as a location, such as "Lake Geneva," you might want to hone in on the exact location you took the photograph. In this case, since I was at a lake and there is no exact address, my only option is to manually move the pin. To do this, follow these steps:

1. Select the pin on the mini-map. Its red head turns yellow.

2. Drag the pin to the proper location. You can use the plus and minus buttons on the map to zoom in or out.

3. When you drop the pin in its new location, it turns red again. You can then click the pin again and change or confirm the name of the location. In the name label, click the check mark to keep the current name or the X to delete it and enter a new one.

Adding Personalized Names to Your Locations

iPhoto lets you add personalized names to locations. So, instead of marking a location as "123 Main Street," you can call it "Mom's House." To change a location's name to something more personal, follow these steps:

1. Select the pin on the mini-map that has the location you want to personalize. Its red head turns yellow.

2. In the name label, enter a nickname for the location.

3. Click the check mark to change the current name to the new one you entered, or click the X to revert to the original name (Figure 6–13).

Figure 6–13. *Adding a nickname to a location*

When you add a personalized name to a location, all photos with that location are updated to reflect the new name.

Removing and Restoring a Photo's Location

iPhoto lets you remove locations from the Places map. Keep in mind that removing a location does not delete the original location data from the photo's EXIF information. The photo's location data will always be encoded in its EXIF data. Removing a location in iPhoto simply removes it from the Places map.

To remove a location, follow these steps:

1. Select the photos or events that include location information.

2. Click the **Info** button in the toolbar to open the Information pane.

3. Click the **Places** header in the Information pane.

4. Select the location's name. If there's more than one location, such as for an entire event, the name says "Multiple locations."

5. Click the X that appears to the right of the name. The location name disappears, and the location is removed from the photo or event.

You can always restore the location to your photos should you choose to do so. This is possible because, as mentioned, iPhoto always keeps the photo's original location data intact in its EXIF information.

To restore a photo's location, follow these steps:

1. Select the photo to which you want to restore the location.

2. From iPhoto's menu bar, choose **Photos ➤ Rescan for Location**.

Managing Places

iPhoto gives you an easy way to manage all your Places locations in, well, one location. You do this through the Manage My Places window. Using Manage My Places, you can quickly see all the personalized places you've added to your photos, rename or delete them, and even fine-tune your locations.

To get started, choose **Window ➤ Manage My Places** from iPhoto's menu bar. The Manage My Places window appears (Figure 6–14).

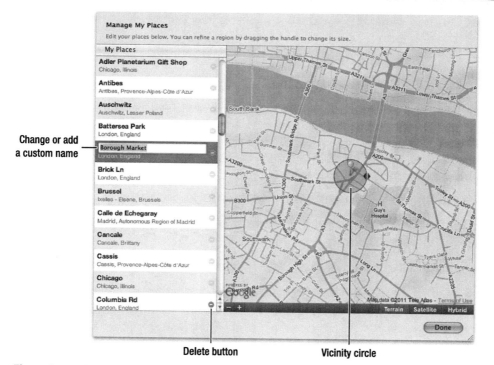

Change or add a custom name

Delete button   Vicinity circle

Figure 6–14. *The Manage My Places window*

To delete a location, follow these steps:

1. Move your mouse over the minus button in the gray circle next to the location you want to delete. The gray minus button turns red. Click it.

2. In the dialog box that appears, click **Delete** to confirm that you want to delete the location. The location is removed from the Places map and any photo that contains the location. Your photos will not be deleted.

To change a place name, follow these steps:

1. Select a place from the list.

2. Double-click its name, and enter a new one. The location's changed name now appears in the pop-up list when you are assigning a location to a photo.

To fine-tune a location on the map, follow these steps:

1. Click and drag the location pin to your desired location. You can use the map's zoom button and different views to hone in on an exact location.

2. (Optional) You can click and hold the edges of the purple vicinity circle to signify that a particular location encompasses a given area. This is handy when labeling certain areas, such as parks or large city blocks.

When you are finished managing your places, click the **Done** button to hide the Manage My Places window.

Using Places to Create Smart Albums

Apple has added a handy shortcut button to the bottom of the Places window that allows you to quickly create smart albums based on the locations you are currently viewing in Places. This is advantageous if you want to create a smart album based on a place or places but don't want to go through the manual steps of creating a location-based smart album as discussed in Chapter 4.

To quickly create a smart album from within Places, follow these steps:

1. Zoom into the region of the map that contains pins for the locations you want to include in the smart album.

2. Click the **Smart Album** button (Figure 6–15) at the bottom of the Places window.

3. A new smart album is created in your Albums list. It's named for the regions it encompasses. You can of course rename it by double-clicking the name and entering a new one.

Figure 6–15. *The Smart Album button in Places*

Once you have created a smart album for a particular region or location, any photos that you add to your photo library from that point on that match that region's or location's latitude-longitude or location data are automatically added to the smart album.

Summary

From automatic geolocation lookup to easy smart album creation to incredible ways to navigate your photos on a global scale, Places is one of the features of iPhoto that quickly becomes most people's favorite. Together with the Events and Faces features, Places completes the trifecta of the novel ways iPhoto allows you to organize and navigate your photos.

In the next chapter, you'll move from organizing and navigating your photos to the other home run feature of iPhoto: photo editing.

Chapter 7

Editing Your Photos

Up until this time you've explored how to navigate and view your photos, which is a big part of iPhoto. Another big part of iPhoto is its simple editing powers. I say "simple" because iPhoto lets you do a lot of complex edits to your pictures with very little work on your part.

In this chapter, you'll learn how to edit your photographs using the tools available to you in the editing window. These tools range from quick fixes to a histogram that lets you make fine-tuned changes to your photos. At the end of the chapter, I also take you through some cool iPhoto tricks that will help you in the editing process.

The Editing Window

Before you get started with some editing, let's take a moment to look at the layout of iPhoto while in Edit mode. To enter Edit mode, select a photograph from your library, and then click the **Edit** button in the iPhoto toolbar. The Edit button resembles a pencil, as shown in Figure 7–1.

Navigation window   Editing tabs

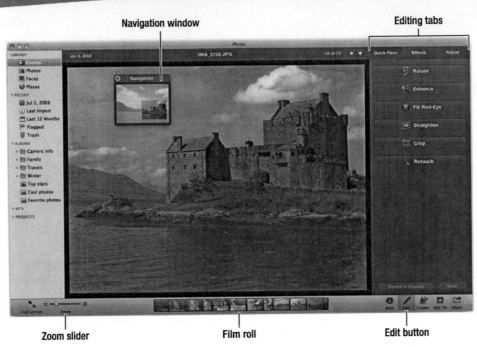

Zoom slider   Film roll   Edit button

Figure 7–1. *The editing window*

As you can see in Figure 7–1, iPhoto retains its similar look and feel while in Edit mode. On the left side you have the source list with all its events, faces, places, and albums, and in the middle you have the selected photo you've chosen to display. However, there are some important new features:

- **Edit button:** This looks like a pencil. Select a photograph you want to edit, and then click the Edit button to enter Edit mode.

- **Film roll:** Use this to navigate the photos in your current album or event. Alternately, you can use the left/right arrow buttons at the top of your screen to move to the next or previous photo.

- **Editing tabs:** The editing tabs are the meat of the editing window and appear at the upper right of iPhoto's edit screen. The tabs are labeled Quick Fixes, Effects, and Adjust. Each tab, when selected, shows you a different range of editing options below it. In Figure 7–1, Quick Fixes is selected, and you can see its tools such as the Rotate and Enhance buttons below it. I go through each tab in detail in this chapter.

- **Zoom slider:** This isn't new; you've seen it before. The Zoom slider simply lets you zoom into a photograph to see a portion of it in more detail. However, when zooming into a photograph in Edit mode, using the Zoom slider causes a small navigation window to appear.

- **Navigation window:** The navigation window pops up on your screen whenever you first zoom into a photograph in Edit mode. What the navigation window does is show you a thumbnail of the full photograph you are zoomed in to.

    The zoomed-in portion is displayed in a clear square in the navigation window, and the rest of the photo that you can't see in iPhoto's main editing window shows up in the navigation window outside of the clear square with a kind of washed-out haze over it.

    You can click and drag the square to pan around, and when you do, the image in iPhoto's editing window pans to match the location of the square. To close the navigation window, click the X in its upper-left corner.

- **Revert to Original button:** I've mentioned in past chapters how iPhoto is a nondestructive editor. That means no matter how many edits you make to your photo, iPhoto always keeps a copy of the original image you imported. If this is your first time editing the photo, you can click the Revert to Original button and quickly return your edited photo from its edited state to the original, imported version no matter how many edits you have performed.

    Note that this button might read Revert to Previous if you've edited the photo during multiple sessions of using iPhoto. Revert to Previous reverts the photo to its last edited state when you closed iPhoto. You can keep clicking Revert to Previous until you see the button change to Revert to Original. Click this, and your photo will revert to its original imported state.

- **Undo button:** Unlike the Revert to Original button, which eliminates all your edits, the Undo button removes the last edit you made. So, if you've fixed red-eye, rotated a photo, and then applied a crop, clicking the Undo button will undo only the crop, not the rotation or the red-eye fix. Click the Undo button again to remove the next edit in the reverse sequence you applied it.

Quick Fixes

If you are using iPhoto to edit your photos, you are likely to be someone who is making simple, fast edits to your favorite pictures. Apple knows this, and that's why it designed iPhoto '11 with a simple three-tab editing layout. The first tab, Quick Fixes, is as simple as they come. This tab, shown in Figure 7–2, allows you to make the six most common edits quickly and efficiently.

Figure 7–2. *The Quick Fixes tab and its edit commands*

Rotate

Rotating a photo is something almost everyone has done or will need to do. Usually when a photo needs to be rotated, it's because you took it in portrait, or vertical, orientation with your camera, but it was imported in the standard landscape, or horizontal, orientation.

To rotate a photo, follow these steps:

1. Select the photo, and click the **Edit** button.

2. On the Quick Fixes tab, click the **Rotate** button. The selected photo is rotated counterclockwise, 90° at a time.

3. Alternately, you can rotate a photo clockwise 90° at a time by holding down the Option key on your keyboard and clicking the **Rotate** button.

You can also rotate a photo by using the keyboard shortcut Command-R or by selecting Photos ➤ Rotate Clockwise or Photos ➤ Rotate Counterclockwise from iPhoto's menu bar.

Enhance

Sometimes you might take a beautifully composed photo but the color may be off or the photo may appear too light or too dark. When this happens, there's no need to panic! iPhoto has a one-click fix for most photos with ailments such as poor saturation or contrast; it's called the Enhance button, and it works almost like magic.

To enhance a photo, follow these steps:

1. Select the photo, and click the **Edit** button.

2. On the Quick Fixes tab, click the **Enhance** button. The selected photo is automatically enhanced based on saturation levels, contrast, exposure, and more.

As you can see in Figure 7–3, enhancing a photo can really bring out details that would normally have remained hidden without doing advanced manual adjustment techniques on it.

Before Enhance   **After Enhance**

Figure 7–3. *The same photo before and after enhancement*

Red-Eye

Ah, red-eye. It's the scourge of photographers everywhere. We're all familiar with red-eye. It's the thing that makes us look like demons in photographs—the red halo that appears in people's eyes that is caused by the makeup of the human eye and the camera's flash. Luckily, most of the cameras on the market today offer built-in red-eye reduction. However, if you still have photos where your friends look like they're about to unleash some heat vision, iPhoto makes it easy to remove their red-eyes.

To remove red-eye, follow these steps:

1. Select the photo of a person with red-eye, and click the **Edit** button.

2. Zoom in on the photograph to the face with the person with red-eye.

3. On the Quick Fixes tab, click the **Fix Red-Eye** button. The red-eye menu expands below the button (see Figure 7–4).

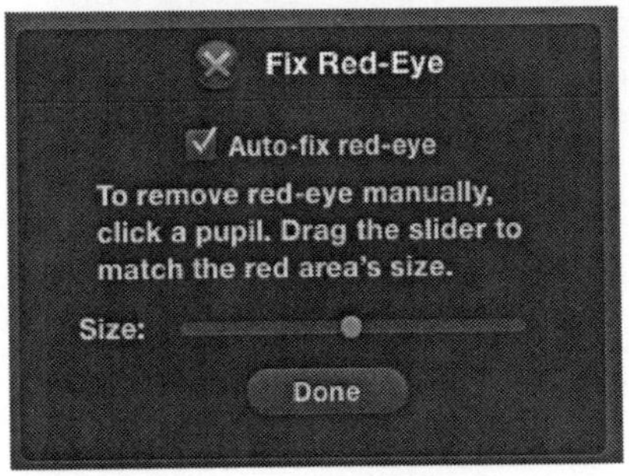

Figure 7–4. *The Fix Red-Eye menu*

4. If iPhoto detects that there are people with red eyes in the photograph, it automatically tries to remove the red-eye. If this doesn't work, uncheck the **Auto-fix red-eye** check box.

5. To remove the red-eye manually, drag the slider until the size of the crosshairs that appear matches the diameter of the person's eyes. Alternatively, you can also change the crosshair size by pressing the left bracket and right bracket ([and]) on your keyboard.

6. Move the red-eye selector over each eye, and click. The red eye is removed (Figure 7–5).

7. Click the **Done** button to exit the Fix Red-Eye menu.

Before Fix Red-eye   **After Fix Red-eye**

Figure 7–5. *Before and after removing red-eye*

Straighten

Sometimes you may have a photograph that's a little crooked. Perhaps you weren't holding the camera perfectly steady, or maybe you put it on a ledge and set the timer so you and all your friends could be in the same photograph, but maybe the ledge wasn't exactly level.

iPhoto lets you easily straighten or level photographs by rotating them slightly—up to 10° in either direction. It's a great feature; just don't use it on any photos of the Leaning Tower of Pisa.

To straighten a photograph, follow these steps:

1. Select the photo to be straightened, and click the **Edit** button.

2. On the Quick Fixes tab, click the **Straighten** button so that its drop-down menu appears and yellow grid lines appear over your photograph (Figure 7–6).

Figure 7–6. *Straightening a photograph*

3. Adjust the slider left or right to straighten the photo. Remember, you can straighten it up to 10° in either direction. Use the yellow lines that are overlaid on the photo as a guide to level ground.

4. When you are finished, click the **Done** button.

Crop

There are tons of reasons you may want to crop your photographs. Perhaps you want to just simply cut out something, such as a stray tree branch or a random stranger who walked into the edge of your photograph. Or you may want to crop a photo to bring attention to a certain part, perhaps making it more artistic. Whatever your reason, iPhoto makes cropping photos painless and easy.

In Figure 7–7, I've cropped a photo to bring attention to the little girl in red boots following her mother on a rainy day in Copenhagen. In the original photo, the girl was located more toward the center, which according to many photographers is an aesthetic no-no for your main subject. I really wanted to make this photo more artistic and spotlight the girl in the red boots, so I decided to crop out the person in the red sweater on the left while at the same time bring the little girl to the more aesthetically pleasing left-third of the screen.

Before Cropping   **After Cropping**

Figure 7–7. *A cropped photo, before and after*

To get the "after" image, I used the crop tool on the Quick Fixes tab.

To crop a photograph, follow these steps:

1. Select the photo to be cropped, and click the **Edit** button.

2. On the Quick Fixes tab, click the **Crop** button so that its drop-down menu appears and the white crop border appears over your photograph (Figure 7–8).

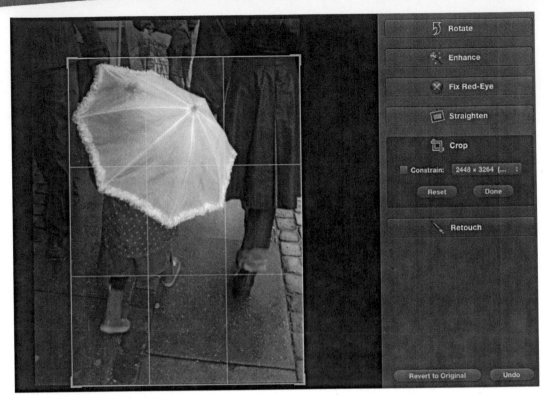

Figure 7–8. *Cropping a photograph*

3. You can drag the border of the crop box in any direction you want. As you do, you'll see white grid lines appear in it, which breaks your photo into thirds. These thirds can help you make aesthetically pleasing crops for your photo.

4. (Optional) You can also check the **Constrain** box to constrain your crop to a specific aspect ratio (the size of your photo, such as 4x6 or 8x10) or shape (such as a square or a DVD cover). To select a specific constraint, choose it from the drop-down menu. This then locks your crop box to the specific shape so that no matter whether you choose to crop just the girl and her umbrella, or even just her single red boot, it would be a perfect 8x10 when viewed or printed, for example.

5. You can click and drag anywhere in the center of the crop box to adjust it to the right spot in the photograph without changing the crop's dimensions. Once you've adjusted the crop box so that it contains just the part of the image you want to retain, click the **Done** button to complete the crop. Clicking the Reset button expands the borders of the crop box back to the boundaries of the original photograph.

Retouch

We all wish we had a magic wand that could quickly remove our real-life blemishes, but until science comes up with such a device, at least take solace in knowing that iPhoto has a magic want of sorts that easily lets you remove blemishes from your photos. This magic wand is called the Retouch button.

As you can see in Figure 7–9, the "before" image shows a man with a small mole on his chin. By using the Retouch button in iPhoto, I've removed that mole with a couple of clicks of the mouse. Pretty nice, huh?

Before Retouching   **After Retouching**

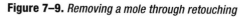

Figure 7–9. *Removing a mole through retouching*

To retouch a photograph, follow these steps:

1. Select the photo to be retouched, and click the **Edit** button.

2. Zoom in on the photograph to the location with the blemish you want to remove. Maybe it's a blemish on the skin or just dust on a photograph that you've scanned into your computer

3. On the Quick Fixes tab, click the **Retouch** button so that its drop-down menu appears. Use the slider to adjust the brush size of the retouch tool (Figure 7–10). Alternatively, you can change the brush size by pressing the left bracket and right bracket ([and]) on your keyboard.

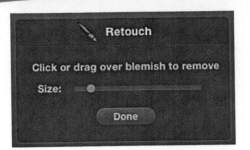

Figure 7–10. *The Retouch drop-down menu and slider*

4. Move the brush over the mark or blemish you want to remove, and then click the mark or drag across it to remove it.

5. (Optional) If the mark or blemish is small, click it a few times. If that doesn't remove it, drag the brush in short strokes to blend it with its surrounding colors.

6. (Optional) You can also copy pixels from another part of the photo and paste them onto the mark or blemish. This effectively covers up the spot you want to eliminate. Press the Option key while you click an area that has the texture you want, and then click the area you want to paste that texture on to.

7. Click the **Done** button to save your changes and exit the Retouch menu.

Effects

For those of you who want to get a little artsy with your photographs, Apple has included a selection of one-click special effects in iPhoto. To access the special effects, go to the Effects tab while in Edit mode. As you can see in Figure 7–11, the Effects tab has a series of round and square buttons, each representing a special effect.

Figure 7–11. *The Effects tab and its special effects*

Round Special-Effect Buttons

There are six round special-effect buttons. The first row involves highlights and shadows. Clicking the Lighten or Darken button adjusts the overall lightness or darkness of your photo one step at a time. Clicking the Contrast button adjusts the contrast, or the difference between light and dark tones, a single step at a time.

The second row of round buttons involves color tinting. Clicking the Warmer button deepens the warm colors, such as yellows, reds, and oranges, in your photo. Clicking the Cooler button deepens the cool colors, such as blues and purples. Clicking the Saturation button adjusts the color intensity of the photo one step at a time.

You can click any of the round buttons as many times as you want. Each time you do, their respective effect is applied again to the photo. This results in a cumulative effect. The more you click the Lighten button, for example, the lighter your photo will get.

To revert to the original photo, click the **Revert to Original** button at the bottom of the Effects tab. To undo just the last applied effect, you can click the **Undo** button at the bottom of the Effects tab.

Square Special-Effect Buttons

As you can see in Figures 7–11 and 7–12, there are nine square special-effects buttons. These buttons apply a specific special effect but in measurable grades, which you can tell by the labels that appear along their bottoms when they are activated.

In Figure 7–12, I have applied several effects to a photograph of a gorilla from the London Zoo. These include sepia, matte, and edge blur. Even without looking at the photo, I can tell I've applied these three specific effects because the labels on the effects buttons tell me so. Sepia is labeled as ON, Matte is at level 2, and Edge Blur is at level 5.

Figure 7–12. *Effects applied to a photo*

I'll briefly list all the square button effects and what they do for clarity's sake:

- **B&W:** Changes photo to black and white. This can be only on or off. If on, Sepia and Antique cannot be used at the same time.

- **Sepia:** Applies a reddish-brown hue to your photo. This can be only on or off. If on, B&W and Antique cannot be used at the same time.

- **Antique:** Gives photos an aged appearance, just like the ones you see at your grandparents'. There are nine levels of Antique. Click the up or down arrows on the labels a step to move through them. If Antique is in use, B&W and Sepia cannot be used at the same time.

- **Matte:** Blurs the edges and corners of a photo in a white oval. There are 24 levels of Matte, each one increasing the diameter of the matte.

- **Vignette:** Darkens the edges and corners of a photo in a black oval. There are 24 levels of Vignette, each one increasing the diameter of the vignette.

- **Edge Blur:** Blurs the edges of a photo like someone has smeared Vaseline on your camera's lens. There are 11 levels of Edge Blur.

- **Fade:** Reduces the color intensity of the photograph as if you've left it outside in the sun for a number of years. There are nine levels of Fade.

- **Boost:** Increases the color intensity of the photograph as if you've printed the same photo directly on top of a copy of it. There are nine levels of Boost.

- **None:** Removes all effects applied to the photo.

With a few exceptions (such as using B&W and Sepia at the same time), all the special effects (round and square) can be applied to a photo in a cumulative fashion to create all sorts of artsy pictures. Have fun with it!

Adjust

For those of you who want to do some manual editing to your photographs, you'll find all the tools you need on the Adjust tab. As you can see in Figure 7–13, the Adjust tab offers a multitude of sliders that allow you to tweak your photos in various ways. I'll go into what each of these sliders do in just a little bit, but first let's talk about what's at the top of the Adjust tab—the histogram.

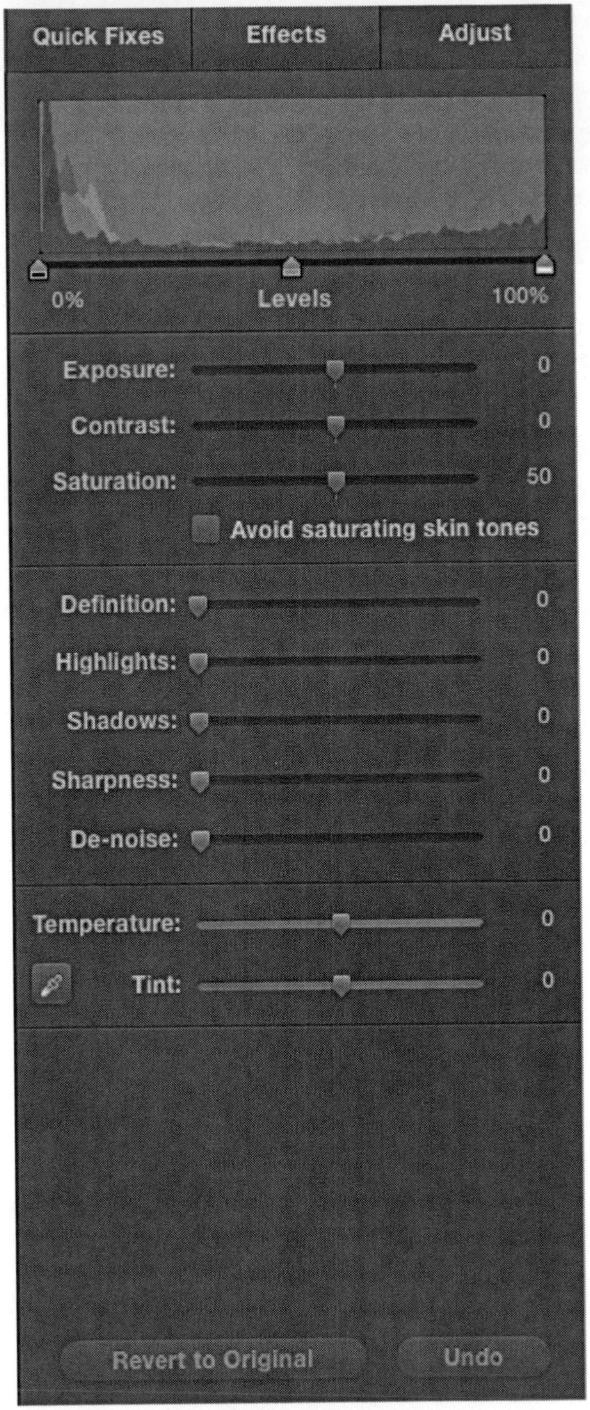

Quick Fixes	Effects	Adjust

0%   Levels   100%

Exposure:		0
Contrast:		0
Saturation:		50

Avoid saturating skin tones

Definition:		0
Highlights:		0
Shadows:		0
Sharpness:		0
De-noise:		0

| Temperature: | | 0 |
| Tint: | | 0 |

Revert to Original   Undo

Figure 7–13. *The Adjust tab and editing options*

Adjusting Your Photos Using the Histogram

Just what is a histogram? Entire books can be written on what a histogram is, but for our purposes, I'll give you a very basic description of what a histogram is and show you how to use it. And don't worry if this seems a little complex. You don't need to understand the histogram to make edits to your photos—just stick with the Quick Fixes and Effects tabs.

A histogram is a graphic representation of the distribution of tones, or light levels, for the three color channels (red, blue, and green) in an image. Black or dark tones are shown in the left of the histogram, mid-tones are shown in the middle, and white or light tones are shown on the right.

Looking at a histogram can instantly tell you whether your photo has good exposure or whether it is underexposed or overexposed. Underexposed photos appear darker than they should be, and overexposed photos appear white, or more "blown-out," than they should be. Remember though, that under- and overexposed photos aren't necessarily bad. Like many things with photography, "good" exposure is somewhat subjective. Maybe you like your photos darker or lighter. Just because a photo is under- or overexposed doesn't mean you *have* to correct it.

In Figure 7–14, you can see what the histograms look like for a photograph with "good" exposure and also photographs that are underexposed and overexposed.

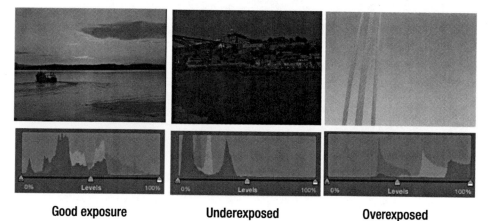

Good exposure   Underexposed   Overexposed

Figure 7–14. *Photographs with "good," under-, and overexposure*

As you can see in the sunset picture, the red, blue, and green colors are spread fairly evenly throughout the histogram. This signifies that the photo has relatively good exposure. In the middle picture, the photograph was taken at night, and you can see it's quite dark. Without even looking at the photo, you could tell it was underexposed just by checking out its histogram. You can see all the colors in the chart are bunched up toward the left, or black, side. In the third photo (it's a shot of three support cables of the Golden Gate Bridge against a blue sky), you'll notice that the colors in the chart are bunched up more to the right, or white side, of the histogram. This means the photograph is overexposed.

Beneath the histogram are three pyramid-shaped markers—one on the left, one in the middle, and one on the right. Below each of those markers is a small bar. The bar on the left is black, the bar in the middle is gray, and the bar on the right is white. These bars signify the black point (tone), mid-tone, or white point (tone) in a photograph.

Ideally—and, again, this is all subjective—you'll want your photos to have a good tone range, with the colors of the chart spread evenly across the histogram. To this end, you can adjust the histogram sliders to clip the ends of the white and black points and adjust the mid-tones—thereby adjusting the photo's light and dark levels—to produce a more balanced photograph.

To do this, drag the black point, mid-tone, or white point sliders underneath the histogram. When you compare the photographs in Figure 7-15 with the ones in Figure 7-14, you can see that I left the first one of the sunset unchanged because I was happy with the light levels. However, for the second photograph, I dragged the white point slider halfway across the histogram in order to lighten the entire image. I can now see much more detail in the river below the bridge, and the overall image is much lighter. For the last photo of the three cables, I adjusted the black point slider and the white point slider to deepen the colors in the photograph. Note that the red cables and the blue sky are much richer in color now.

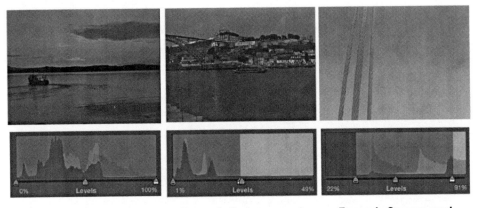

Unchanged Good exposure   Formerly Underexposed   Formerly Overexposed

Figure 7-15. *Photographs that have had their light levels (or tones) adjusted using the histogram sliders*

Remember, using the histogram takes practice. The more you play with the sliders, the better you'll get at manually adjusting the tones in your photographs. But also remember that you don't need to use the histogram at all if you don't want to do so. You can adjust all the tones in your photograph by simply clicking the **Enhance** button on the Quick Fixes tab. While manually adjusting the histogram sliders gives you greater control, most iPhoto users will probably find the Enhance button is more than enough for them.

NOTE: Keep in mind that you can quickly undo your last edit by clicking the Undo button in the editing window. You can also revert to the original copy of the photograph you are editing—no matter how many edits you've applied—by clicking the Revert to Original button, so don't worry about messing up your photos by playing around with the histogram. You can always undo what you have done.

Below the histogram slider, the remainder of iPhoto's Adjust editing tools consist of more sliders. iPhoto has these sliders divided into three individual sections, so let's look at them one section at a time.

Adjusting Exposure, Contrast, and Saturation

The first group of sliders are the Exposure, Contrast, and Saturation sliders (Figure 7–16). There's also a check box regarding skin tones.

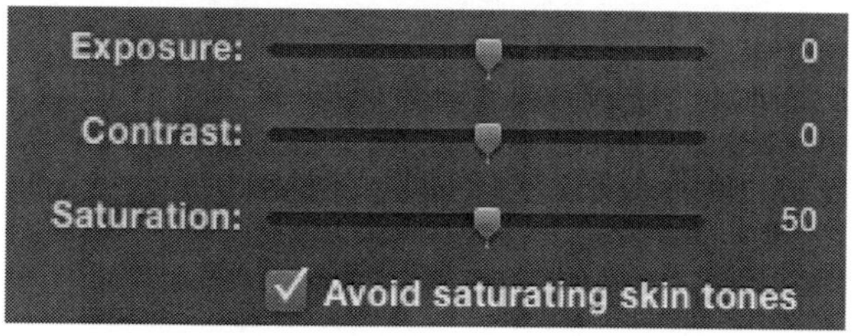

Figure 7–16. *Exposure, contrast, and saturation sliders*

- **Exposure:** Moving this slider adjusts the overall lightness of a photograph. Unlike the sliders directly below the histogram chart, which adjust individual light tones, mid-tones, or dark tones, the Exposure slider adjusts all tones evenly. Drag it to the right of the 0 marker to increase a photo's brightness, or drag it to the left of the 0 marker to decrease its brightness.

- **Contrast:** The contrast of a photo is the amount of difference between the light and dark areas in it. In a high-contrast photo, you'll see a sharper divide between light and dark. In a low-contrast photo, the divide won't be as jarring (see Figure 7–17).

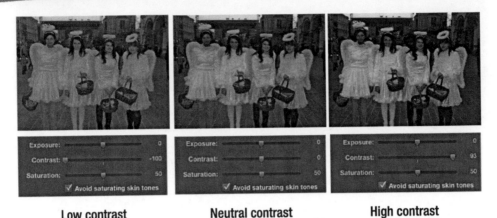

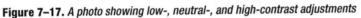

Low contrast   Neutral contrast   High contrast

Figure 7–17. *A photo showing low-, neutral-, and high-contrast adjustments*

- **Saturation:** Adjusting the Saturation slider changes the color richness, or intensity, of the photograph. By default, the Saturation slider is set at 50. This is neutral. By dragging the slider to the left, you'll be decreasing the intensity of the colors in your photo. If you drag the slider all the way to the left, down to 0, the photo will become black and white. Conversely, dragging the slider to the right will increase the intensity of the colors of your photo. If you drag the slider all the way to 100, the colors in your photo will look quite nuclear, as if they were radiating light.

- **Avoid Saturating Skin Tones:** With this check box selected, any changes you make to the color intensity of your photograph using the Saturation slider do not affect any skin tones in your photograph. This is a great feature because it allows you to avoid giving the people in your photos horrible orange tans when you increase the saturation of a photo (Figure 7–18).

Avoid saturating skin tones checked   Avoid saturating skin tones unchecked

Figure 7–18. *The same photo with saturation boosted but with Avoid Saturating Skin Tones checked in the left image and unchecked in the right. Note the orange skin in the right photo.*

Adjusting Definition, Highlights, Shadows, Sharpness, and Noise

The second group of sliders (Figure 7–19) allows you to adjust highlights and shadows in your photographs as well as manipulate the amount of details, grain, and focus in them. Once you have adjusted your contrast and exposure, using these adjustment tools can really make your photos pop!

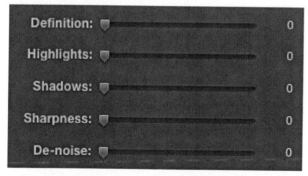

Figure 7–19. *Control grain, highlights, and focus in your photos.*

- **Definition:** This slider allows you to bring out the details in a photograph. Just like a person with six-pack abs is called "defined," this slider allows you to chisel away soft lines in your photographs to make impressions stand out.

- **Highlights:** Use this slider to reduce the brightness of highlights in your photo. In other words, it darkens bright areas (such as a bright sky) so you can see more detail in them (such as wisps of clouds).

- **Shadows:** This is the opposite of the Highlights slider. This increases the brightness of shadows in your photo so you can see more detail in a dark area. For example, a person in your photo might be wearing a black shirt. In the photo, the black shirt might look like a solid, almost formless, mass of black. Using the shadows slider, you can bring out the details in the shirt like the ripple is its fabric.

- **Sharpness:** To see the benefit of the Sharpness slider, it helps to be zoomed in on your photograph to something that has defined edges, like a window frame. When you edit a digital photo, the adjustments you make to its contrast or exposure can sometimes cause a soft, or blurred, edge to lined objects in your photo. You can use the Sharpness slider to fix the blurred edges so they show up more crisply in photos. Note that you cannot use the Sharpness slider to fix a photo that was taken out of focus.

- **De-noise:** If you've ever taken a photograph outside at night, you've seen noise in your images. Noise is distortion. It's the little blips and specs that show up on your digital photos and appear almost as if they were dust or colored confetti. You can use the De-noise slider to minimize those specs of digital dust.

Again, the best way to learn to use these tools is to just play around with them. In Figure 7–20 you can see the "before" and "after" versions of a photo I applied the previous settings to.

Before   **After**

Figure 7–20. *Before and after shots of adjusting the definition, highlights, and noise in a photograph*

In the photograph in Figure 7–20 I first used the Definition slider to bring out details in the white scarf and waves in the river. I then used the Highlights slider to darken the highlights in the sky, which brought out more clouds. Next, I used the Shadows slider to lighten the shadows in the trees on the riverbank. This allowed me to see more details in their leaves. Then I zoomed in on Big Ben in the background to restore some sharpness to its edges that was lost when adjusting the first three edits. Finally, I slightly adjusted the De-noise slider to remove a few minor artifacts in the image (which are not noticeable in the "before" image on the printed page of this book).

Adjusting Temperature, Tint, and Color Cast

When you hear temperature, you usually think about the weather outside. But in a photograph, temperature refers to *color temperature*, or the warmth and coolness of the colors in the photograph. *Tint* refers to the reds and greens in your photo. Taken together, temperature and tint are called *color cast*.

Photos in which you might want to adjust the color cast are photos that are shot indoors. Many times these photos might have an orange hue to them because of the lighting in your house. Alternatively, photos could look too blue if you took them in shadow. Also, an entire photo can be tinted blue or orange if there is a lot of that particular color in the photograph.

If you need to adjust the color cast of a photograph, you can do so easily using the eyedropper tool shown in Figure 7–21.

Temperature: ——————————————————— 0

Tint: ——————————————————— 0

Figure 7–21. *The Temperature and Tint sliders along with the color cast eyedropper tool*

To adjust the color cast of a photo using the eyedropper tool, follow these steps:

1. Click the eyedropper tool. Your cursor will turn into crosshairs.

2. Move the crosshairs over your photo, and find an area of the photo with a neutral gray or white point in the photo to remove its color cast. The color tint and temperature change automatically. You can now deselect the eyedropper tool or use it to click another location of the photograph to change the color temperature and tint again if you so desire.

In Figure 7–22 notice how that in the "before" shot, the water took on the same blue hue of the sky. I used the eyedropper tool to select a white point on a cloud in the photograph. This told iPhoto to color balance the photo to neutral based on that white point. The result is the same blue skies but a more correct color tone for the water (which was more blue-green) and the sand on the beach (which was darker).

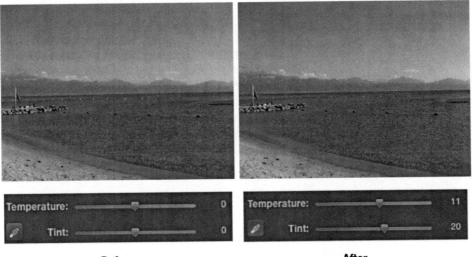

Before   **After**

Figure 7–22. *Before and after of the same photo using the eyedropper color cast tool*

If you want to adjust the temperature or tint of a photograph manually, you can do so easily using the Temperature and Tint sliders shown in Figure 7–21. Do not select the eyedropper tool; instead, drag the sliders until you get the right color cast you want for your photograph.

Cool iPhoto Editing Tricks

iPhoto has a number of cool little tricks that a lot of people don't know about. I've decided to describe them all here so you can learn about them in a single place. Many of these tricks are very simple, but they go a long way toward helping you edit your photos.

Copy and Paste Edit Adjustments from One Photo to Another

Let's say you've spent half an hour using the Adjust sliders correcting a photo to make the colors and exposures just perfect. That's a big feat, but you want to apply those same changes to other similar photos (such as multiple shots of the same beach taken at the same time) without having to go through all the manual adjustments again.

Well, you're in luck! You can! Here's how:

1. After you've adjusted a photo, from iPhoto's menu bar select Edit ➤ Copy Adjustments.

2. Next, select another photo that is similar to the one you have adjusted. Usually the easiest way to do this is by using the film roll at the bottom of the editing window (see Figure 7–1). The film roll is easiest because usually similar photos are next to each other because that's the way you took them, sequentially, with your camera.

3. Once the other photo is selected, from iPhoto's menu bar select Edit ➤ Paste Adjustments and—*voila!*—all your adjustments are applied from the first photo to the second. You can then continue tweaking the adjustments on the second photo as you wish.

Pretty cool, huh?

Duplicating Your Photos

Editing your photos is awesome, but sometimes you want to keep the original copy and have an edited copy. You can easily do this by using the Duplicate Photo command in iPhoto. This creates two copies of the photo in your iPhoto library, so only the copy you choose to edit is changed.

To duplicate a photo, follow these steps:

1. Select the photo you want to duplicate. Generally it's a good idea to duplicate it before you've started any edits.

2. From iPhoto's menu bar, choose Photos ➤ Duplicate. You can also press Command-D on your keyboard.

3. The duplicated photo appears next to the original photo in the album or event you duplicated it in. A "Version 2" is appended to its file name. For example, for an original photograph with the name "IMG_0636.JPG," the duplicate has the name "IMG_0636.JPG – Version 2."

Quickly Review Your Original Preedited Photograph

Sometimes when editing a photograph, you wonder just how far you've come. What does it look like now compared to how it first looked? Well, you can of course click the Revert to Original button, but then you've lost all your edits. You can also duplicate the original photograph, but this would have to have been done *before* you started editing it. Even if you did, you would have to then navigate to the duplicate photo in your iPhoto Library.

Not to worry; with the press of a single button you can quickly see how the photo you are editing originally looked. That button is the Shift key on your keyboard. Press it at any time to see what the original photo looked like. Release the Shift key to return to the edited photo. This is a great shortcut that allows you to see whether your editing is heading you in the right direction (does the photo look better now after the edits, or did it look better before?).

Compare Two or More Photos

With the advent of digital cameras it seems natural to record multiple takes of the same image. We quickly rattle off endless shots of our child in front of his first birthday cake like it's going out of style. That's great for recording memories, but when it comes to deciding which of those shots to take the time to edit—since they are all so similar—it can cause a bit of a headache.

Luckily iPhoto lets you quickly compare two or more shots at once. This allows you to see them all at the same time and choose which one you want to edit.

To compare two or more photos, follow these steps:

1. Select two or more photos you want to view or edit. Click and drag the selection box around the photos if they are next to each other, or hold down the Command key on your keyboard and click each photo you want to compare so it is highlighted in a yellow box.

2. Click the **Edit** button in the toolbar. The photos you have selected to compare appear (see Figure 7–23).

3. Select one of the photos so it is highlighted in a white box. You can then proceed to edit the selected photo. To select a new photo to edit from those you are comparing, simply click it so a white box appears around it.

4. To remove one of the compared photos, select it, and then click the X in its upper-left corner to remove it from view.

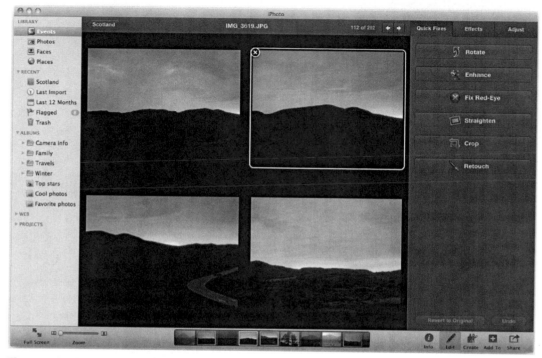

Figure 7–23. *Four photos being compared*

Contextual Menu Shortcuts

While editing a selected photo, you can right-click it to bring up a contextual menu of quick shortcuts. These shortcuts are more ways of carrying out certain edit commands that I have discussed in this chapter.

As you can see in Figure 7–24, the shortcuts include rotating, copying and pasting adjustments, duplicating photos, and more. Also in Figure 7–24 you'll notice an Open in External Editor shortcut. I haven't talked about that in this chapter, but I'll address it in Chapter 10.

Figure 7–24. *Contextual menu editing shortcuts*

Zooming Tricks

I talked about zooming in on photos while in Edit mode earlier in this chapter, but I didn't want to close this chapter out without mentioning a couple zoom tricks built into iPhoto. You can use the 1, 2, and 0 keys on your keyboard to quickly zoom into and out of a photograph while editing it. These number keys also perform differently depending on whether your cursor is on the photo or you have moved it to another part of your screen so it is not over your photograph.

When the cursor is not on your photograph, you can do the following:

- Press the 1 key on your keyboard to zoom into the *center* of the photo and view it at 100 percent.

- Press the 2 key on your keyboard to zoom into the *center* of the photo and view it at 200 percent.

- Press the 0 key on your keyboard to zoom back out.

With the cursor over a specific part of your photo that you want to zoom in on, you can do the following:

- Move the cursor to the spot you want to zoom in on, and press the 1 key on your keyboard to zoom into the exact spot your cursor is on in the photo and view it at 100 percent.

- Move the cursor to the spot you want to zoom in on, and press the 2 key on your keyboard to zoom into the exact spot your cursor is on in the photo and view it at 200 percent.

- Press the 0 key on your keyboard to zoom back out.

Summary

So, that's editing in iPhoto '11! As you can see, iPhoto provides you with the tools you need to edit your photos no matter whether you want the quick fix, are the artsy type, or want to delve into more advanced photo editing. iPhoto's editing tools are an invaluable part of the program that allow you to make your photos even richer and more exciting. Take your time and get used to them; you'll be glad you did, especially the next time you see a blemish on your face that you want to remove.

In the next chapter, we'll discuss all the various keepsakes you can create from within iPhoto including books, cards, and calendars.

Creating Keepsakes: Books, Cards, Calendars, and Slideshows

Once you have all your photos organized and edited, you'll most likely want to share them with people and not keep them all to yourself. Luckily, iPhoto '11 makes sharing fun and easy. iPhoto lets you share your photos in two ways: electronically and physically.

In this chapter, you'll learn all the physical ways to share your photos by creating photo keepsakes such as books, calendars, and cards that you can create and give to your friends and family. Although they're not physical entities, slideshows will be discussed in this chapter for completeness. Slideshows are grouped in the menu that allows you to create all those cool books, calendars, and cards—the Create menu.

Keepsakes and the Create Menu

iPhoto '11 has a single powerful button that makes creating keepsakes easy and fun. This button, appropriately enough, is called the Create button. You can see it in Figure 8–1. It looks like a silhouette of a bottle of glue and a scissors. If this button looks familiar, it's because I talked about it in Chapter 4 when you learned how to create albums.

When you click the Create button, the Create pop-up menu will appear (Figure 8–1). In it you will see five options. There is of course the Album option, which lets you create a new album (see Chapter 4); then below the Album option, you have four additional ones: Book, Card, Calendar, and Slideshow. This chapter will show you how to create all four types of these keepsakes.

Figure 8–1. *The Create menu*

Before you delve into creating keepsakes, you'll briefly learn about how iPhoto displays your keepsakes. As you can see in Figure 8–2, there are some specific areas that deal with keepsakes.

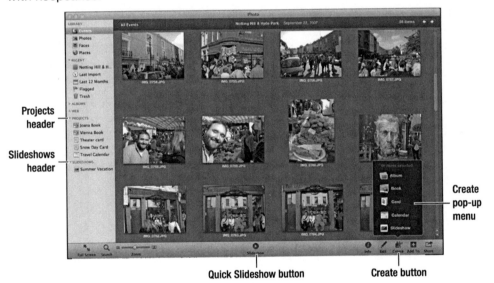

Figure 8–2. *Keepsakes in iPhoto*

■ **Create button and pop-up menu:** Selecting Book, Card, Calendar, or Slideshow in the Create pop-up menu takes you to that keepsake's theme chooser screen. You can also create a new keepsake by selecting File ➤ New and then Book, Card, Calendar, or Slideshow from iPhoto's menu bar.

■ **Projects and Slideshows headers:** These are located in iPhoto's source list and show you all the keepsakes you have created. Collectively, I refer to all of iPhoto's creation menu items as keepsakes, but Apple has decided to segregate slideshows from books, cards, and calendars. This results in Books, Cards, and Calendars being placed under the Projects heading and Slideshows being under the Slideshows heading.

■ **Instant Slideshow button:** Clicking this button quickly displays a slideshow of the selected photos or album. The resulting slideshow appears immediately on your screen and is not saved as a keepsake in the Slideshows header in iPhoto's source list. I'll talk about both kinds of slideshows later in this chapter.

You can view any keepsakes you've created by clicking them in the source list. You can also double-click them to change their name.

> **NOTE:** Once you know how to create one keepsake—a book, for instance—you know how to create them all. In this chapter, I'll go through creating all the different kinds of keepsakes, but I'll start by focusing on books since they are the most popular. I'll then cover cards, calendars, and slideshows, and I'll note any of the major differences in creating those keepsakes.

Creating a Book

To get started creating a book, the best thing to do is group all the images you want to use in the book into an album or an event. You don't need to put all your images in one location, but doing so makes your workflow easier.

1. Once you have chosen the images you want to use in a book, select them (either individually or as an album or event), and then click the Create button in iPhoto's toolbar. From the pop-up menu that appears, select Book. The theme chooser screen appears, as shown in Figure 8–3.

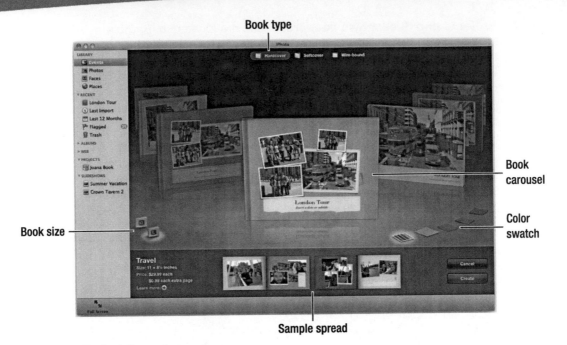

Figure 8–3. *The book theme chooser screen*

The book theme chooser has four main interactive elements:

- **Book carousel:** This is a representation of the books available to you. You'll note that your photos have already been applied to the covers. The book carousel contains a number of book themes. Each theme provides you with a different look and layout depending on the one you choose. Some examples of book themes are Travel, Picture Book, Journal, and Photo Essay. Click the books to rotate through the carousel.

- **Book type:** Click to choose the type of book you want to create. Your options include hardcover, softcover, or wire-bound.

- **Book size:** Click to choose from between a large or extra-large book size.

- **Color swatch:** Click the different color squares to change a book's color scheme.

2. As you change themes and other selections such as type, size, and color swatches, the image of the books in the carousel change in real time to show you a preview of what the book is going to look like when printed. Also, as you make your selections, the bottom portion of the theme selector updates to show you a sample spread of the pages inside the book. The sample spread also lists the size and price of each book.

3.   When you are happy with the theme and style chosen, click the **Create** button. This assembles your pictures into a book.

All Pages Screen

Once you click the Create button in the theme selector, you are taken to the All Pages screen (Figure 8–4). The All Pages screen shows you the exact layout of your book from front cover to back cover.

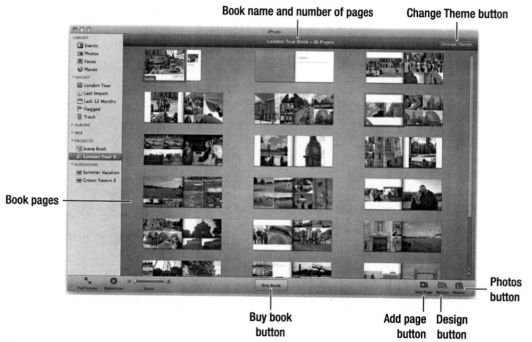

Figure 8–4. *The All Pages screen*

At the top of the All Pages screen, the name of your book project and the number of pages in the book are displayed. You can also click the **Change Theme** button to return to the theme chooser screen if you don't like the overall theme of the book.

In the main body of the All Pages screen are your book's pages. You can click and drag pages around to sort them into the order you want, or you can simply leave everything as it is and click the **Buy Book** button. However, if you want to do some fine-tuning with your book, the three toolbar buttons in the lower right of the screen enable you to make any changes you want.

Changing the Layout of Individual Pages

iPhoto allows you to manipulate the individual layout of your book's pages. There are so many options that I would need a 2,000-page book to go through them all. With that in mind, let's look at some of the page layout options. Once you learn the basics, you can explore all the options on your own.

To change the layout of an individual page in your assembled book, follow these steps:

1. Double-click the page you want to change. The selected page is displayed in iPhoto's window. A navigator window also appears. This shows you which part of your two-page book spread you are zoomed into. You can use the Zoom slider in iPhoto's toolbar to zoom further in or out.

2. Click the **Design** button to open the Design pane (see Figure 8–5).

Figure 8–5. *Editing a page's layout*

3. Click a color style under the Background header in the Design pane to change the background page color.

4. From the layout header, select the drop-down menu to choose how many photos you want to show on the selected page, and then select one of the white layout squares that feature different layout patterns. When you select one, your images will rearrange on the page to match the new pattern. You can then drag and drop images on top of each other to switch their positions.

As you can see from Figure 8–6, you can choose from a number of page layouts. The possibilities really are almost endless.

```
    1 Photo
    2 Photos
    3 Photos
    4 Photos
    5 Photos
✓ 6 Photos
    7 Photos
    8 Photos
    9 Photos
   10 Photos
   12 Photos
   13 Photos
   16 Photos

   Text Page
   Map
   Spread
   Blank

   Custom
```

Figure 8–6. *Almost limitless page layout options*

You aren't limited to just rearranging your photos and their layout on an individual page. You can also edit and manipulate individual photos on the page.

To edit an individual photo on a page, follow these steps:

1. Double-click the page you want to change. The selected page is displayed in iPhoto's window.

2. Click the **Design** button to open the Design pane.

3. Now click the photo you want to edit. As you can see in Figure 8–7, the Design pane has changed to show individual edit controls.

Figure 8–7. *Editing a photo on a page*

4. From the Borders header, select a border to apply to your photo. From the Effects header, choose from adding black and white, sepia, or antique filters to your photo. You can also click the Edit Photo button to be taken to the regular edit mode in iPhoto for that image (see Chapter 7).

5. You'll also notice that a Zoom slider has appeared for the selected photo. You can use it to zoom in or out of the photo and then click and drag the photo around to place it in your desired position.

> **NOTE:** When creating a new book based on a selection of photos (such as an event or album), iPhoto automatically populates the book's pages with the photos from that album. It doesn't do this randomly, however. iPhoto features your higher-rated photos as larger images on the page and also knows to center images with faces in them, so your girlfriend's face, for example, isn't going to get cut off in the photograph.

Add Additional Pages and Photos to Your Book

Just because you first assembled your book based on a selection of photos doesn't mean you can't add extra pages of photos to your book.

To add a new blank page and then add photos to it, follow these steps:

1. Click the **Add Page** button (Figure 8–4). A new blank page appears (Figure 8–8).

Figure 8–8. *Adding a blank page*

2. Select the blank page, and a pop-up design menu appears that lets you choose the layout and background color of the page. Note that this pop-up menu (shown in Figure 8–8) offers you the same options as the Design pane. As usual, in iPhoto there are multiple ways to do the same thing.

3. Once you have chosen the design of the new page, click the **Photos** button in the iPhoto toolbar. This opens the Photos pane (Figure 8–8).

4. From the Photos pane you can choose to show all the photos in your current book project, only the placed photos, or only the unplaced photos, or you can choose to show the photos from your last viewed event, last camera import, last 12 months, or ones that have been flagged (Figure 8–9).

Whatever option you choose, you can then scroll through the available photos in the Photos pane and simply drag them to place them on the new page. Note that any photos with a check mark on them are already being used in your current project. This doesn't mean you can't use them twice; just know that they have already been used.

Figure 8–9. *Choosing which photos to view in the Photos pane*

Clearing and Autofilling All Photos in Your Book

By default when you create a new project from a selected album or event, iPhoto arranges all the photos in your book. As you've seen, you can easily manipulate and change the layout of entire pages or individual photos. However, you can also wipe the entire book clean and start new. To do this, follow these steps:

1. Click the **Photos** button in the toolbar.

2. At the bottom of the Photo pane are two buttons: Autoflow and Clear Placed Photos (Figure 8–10).

3. Click **Clear Placed Photos**, and all the photos are removed from your book.

4. To add the photos again manually, click and drag them from the Photos pane to the pages of your choosing.

5. If you decide iPhoto had laid out the photos better than you did, you can click the Autoflow button, and iPhoto automatically fills the remaining pages with photos you have not used.

Figure 8–10. *The Autoflow and Clear Placed Photos buttons*

Formatting Text in Books

Many book themes allow you to add text to pages. To enter text, find a page with a text field, click inside it, and start typing. After you've entered your text, you have several options for formatting it.

The quick way to format text is to simply select what you have written and then choose options from the drop-down menu that appears in the text format pop-up menu (Figure 8–11).

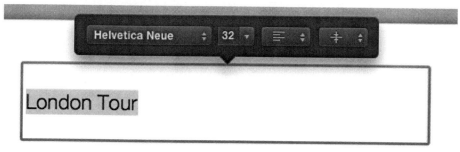

Insert a description of your book (You can write several sentences describing you photos.)

Figure 8–11. *The quick format text menu*

From the quick format menu, you can change font, text size, horizontal, and vertical alignments.

However, as I've mentioned several times, there's more than one way to do the same thing in iPhoto. When you are editing text, clicking the Design button opens the Design pane and displays all of the additional text-formatting features iPhoto offers.

As you can see in Figure 8–12, the text-formatting pane offers you a complete assortment of fonts, text sizes, text colors, alignments, columns, kerning, and spacing options all from an easily accessible menu.

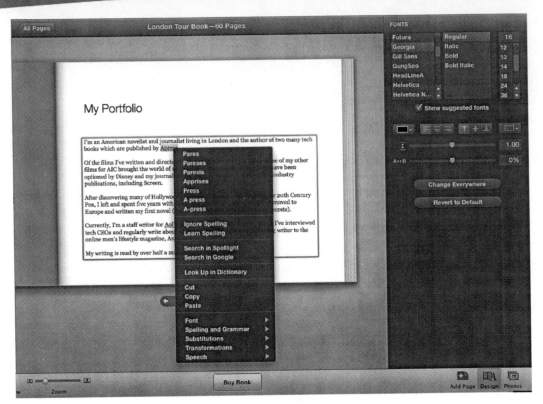

Figure 8–12. *The text-formatting pane*

While editing text, you also have a wide array of contextual menu options just like you do in a word processor. You can see these options in the black box in Figure 8–12. They include checking the spelling, suggesting words, copying and pasting, and looking up a word in the dictionary, among other tools.

Two important buttons to keep in mind while editing text are Change Everywhere and Revert to Default. Clicking Change Everywhere applies your selected text settings to all other text fields of the same default style in your book. Revert to Default undoes your selected text settings and applies the book theme's default text settings to your text.

Using Maps in Books

Out of the myriad layouts you can choose to have in your book, perhaps one of the coolest is the map layout. Choosing a map layout lets you add a map to your book and mark the locations where your photos were taken. This is an excellent feature to include in a book of travel photos.

As you can see in Figure 8–13, you have several setting choices when adding a map. The Style menu allows you to choose between seven different map styles. Below that, in the Location menu, you can manually add locations to the map, or if your photos are tagged with GPS data, their locations show up automatically. Drag the locations up or down in the Places list, and then apply a connection line to visually show the path you took between the locations. You can zoom in and out of the map using the pop-up zoom slider and then drag the map around so it shows only the area you want.

The check boxes under the Show heading enable you to show or hide other details on the map. These include a title, place markers, a compass, and more.

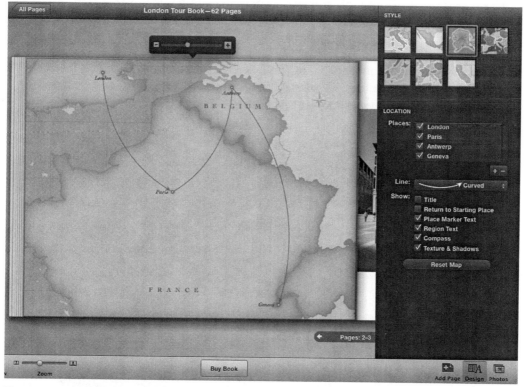

Figure 8–13. *Adding a map to your book*

When you have finished assembling a book to your liking, you are ready to purchase it. I'll discuss how to purchase your completed keepsake projects later in this chapter.

Creating a Card

Once you've learned how to create a book in iPhoto, you pretty much know how to create a card and calendar too. Apple wisely chose to make the creation process and tools the same. Before I jump into creating cards, I do want to point out one of the new card types introduced in iPhoto '11—the letterpress card.

Traditionally, custom cards created and ordered through software applications such as iPhoto have all used modern printing techniques. This means they've all been printed using standard cardstock send through digital printers. With the introduction of letterpress cards in iPhoto '11, however, Apple has blended cutting-edge digital printing techniques with centuries-old printing methods.

When you order a letterpress card, the theme you choose is physically embossed into the cardstock paper. This means the recipient of the card can actually feel the bumps and recesses of the design. Your photos are then digitally printed into the embossed cardstock, creating a unique look and feel. Letterpress cards are really quite spectacular to behold, and each one you order also comes with a matching embossed envelope.

To create a card, follow these steps:

1. Choose the image you want to use from your iPhoto Library, and click the **Create** button in iPhoto's toolbar. From the pop-up menu that appears, select **Card**. The theme chooser screen will appear, as shown in Figure 8–14.

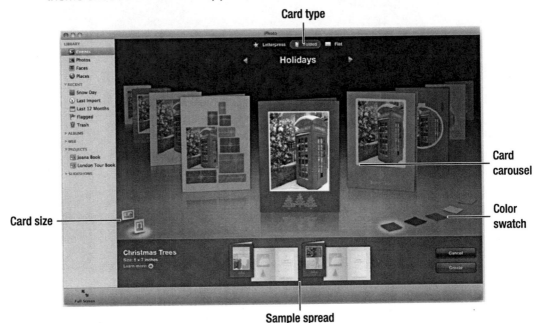

Figure 8–14. *The card theme chooser screen*

2. As you can see from Figure 8–14, the theme chooser for cards is much the same as the theme chooser for books (Figure 8–3). As with books, select the type of card you want to create by clicking the card type at the top of the screen.

3. Next, navigate through the card carousel, and select the card design you want to use.

4. Continue choosing the card size and color swatches, and then click the **Create** button once you are ready to assemble the card.

Personalizing Your Cards

Once you've clicked the Create button in the card theme chooser window, the card layout screen appears (Figure 8–15). Here you can make changes to your card's layout—such as changing the colors or switching between horizontal and vertical landscapes. You can also enter custom text and stylize the text using the text style options in the Design pane.

Personalizing the layout of a card is like a simple version of a book. There are not a lot of options, and once you know how to make a book, creating a card is a snap.

When you have finished personalizing your card, you can click the **Buy Card** button. I'll talk about the buying process for books, cards, and calendars later in this chapter.

Figure 8–15. *The card layout screen*

Creating a Calendar

Believe it or not, creating a calendar is even easier than creating a card—at least when it comes to the theme chooser step. To get started creating a calendar, the best thing to do is first group the images you want to use in the calendar into one location, just like you did when creating a book. This single location could be an album or an event. You don't need to put all your images in one location, but doing so just makes it easier for your workflow.

1. Once you have the images you want to use in a calendar, select them (either individually or as an album or event), and click the **Create** button in iPhoto's toolbar. From the pop-up menu that appears, select **Calendar**. The theme chooser screen appears, as shown in Figure 8–16.

Calendar carousel

Sample spread

Figure 8–16. *The calendar theme chooser screen*

2. As you can see in Figure 8–16, the only option you have to choose from when creating a calendar is which theme to use. You can't modify calendars by size or color swatches like you can with books and cards. Navigate through the calendar carousel until you find the right calendar theme, and then click the **Create** button once you are ready to assemble the calendar.

3. When you click the **Create** button, a dialog box pops up on the screen asking you to choose the settings for your calendar, as shown in Figure 8–17.

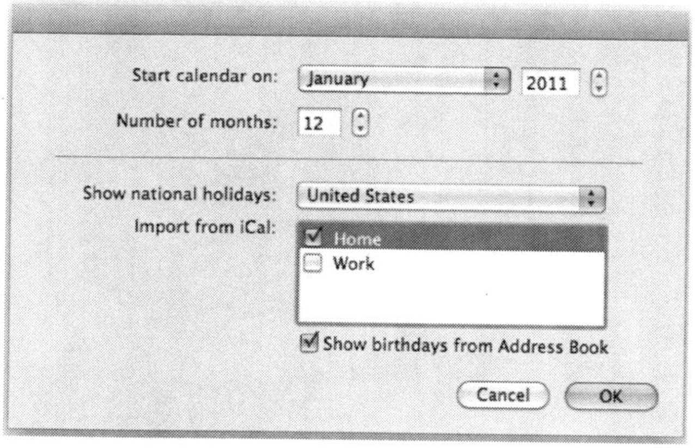

Figure 8–17. *Calendar settings*

The calendar settings dialog box is where you determine which data gets included in your calendar.

- **Start Calendar On:** Choose the month and year you want your calendar to start on.

- **Number of months:** Decide how many months you want your calendar to contain. You don't always have to do 12; sometimes an 18–month calendar is nice.

- **Show National Holidays:** Select the country for which to display the national holidays of.

- **Import from iCal:** Here you can select to import events from your iCal calendars on your computer. iCal is Mac OS X's built-in calendar software. Check a particular iCal calendar's box to include it in your iPhoto calendar.

- **Show Birthdays from Address Book:** If you check this, any birthdays you have recorded for people in your address book show up on your calendar.

4. Once you have selected your data settings, click the OK button to be taken to the calendar layout screen.

Personalizing Your Calendar Layout

The calendar layout screen displays thumbnails of each page of your calendar. Just like with the All Pages view when creating a book, you can drag and drop the picture sections of calendar months to rearrange the images in the calendar.

As shown in Figure 8–18, while in calendar layout view, the Design pane gives you access to all your calendar data settings. You can choose any of the data settings by altering them in the Design pane.

Figure 8–18. *Calendar layout view*

Personalizing Individual Months

To edit and tweak individual calendar months to your liking, double-click any calendar page to bring up the calendar page edit screen (Figure 8–19). Here, just like with books and cards, you can change the background color of a calendar page, alter the layout of the photographs, and, by using the Photos pane, replace the images on that specific calendar page.

Figure 8–19. *Personalizing individual months*

Adding Text or Photos to Specific Dates

One really cool feature of calendars is the ability to add text or a photo to any specific date square on the calendar. This is handy when you want to specify a certain event, such as an anniversary or the beginning of your trip to Europe.

To add text to a date square, follow these steps:

1. From the calendar page layout screen (Figure 8–19), double-click any date square. A date square pop-up window will appear (Figure 8–20).

2. Enter whatever text you want.

3. Use the font-formatting menu at the bottom of the date square window to format your text, or use the text-formatting options available in the Design pane.

4. When you are done editing and formatting your text, click the X in the upper-left corner of the date square window to close it. You'll be able to view your text on the calendar now.

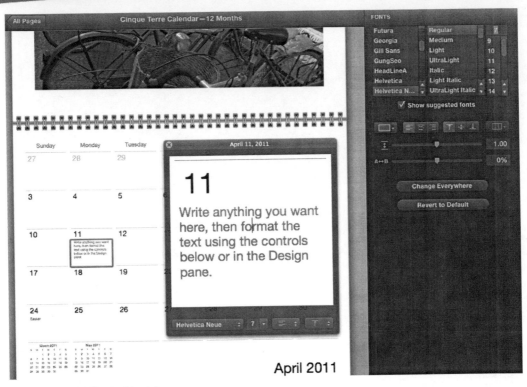

Figure 8-20. *Adding text to date squares*

You can also fill date squares with photos. Perhaps you want to signify your child's birthday with her photograph, or maybe you just want to spice up the calendar page by adding random photos throughout the month.

To add a photo to a date square, follow these steps:

1. From the calendar page layout screen, click the **Photos** button so your photos are displayed in the pane next to the calendar.

2. Choose the photo you want to fill a date square with, and then drag and drop it onto the date square. If the photo fits into the square as you like it, you're done. If not, click the photo inside the date square to open the date square pop-up window (Figure 8-21).

Figure 8–21. *Adding photos to date squares*

3. From the date square pop-up window, you can move the slider below the image to zoom in or out and then drag the zoomed image around to place it in the date square how you want it.

4. It's also possible to add a caption to the image. Note that the caption isn't overlaid on the image in the date square; it is placed in the date square above or below, or to the left or right, of the date square with the photo in it. An arrow next to the caption points toward the photo it is referencing.

5. When you are done editing and formatting your date square photo, click the *X* in the upper-left corner of the date square window to close it.

Buying Your Keepsakes

You need to buy the keepsakes once you are done creating them. You can print them yourself using iPhoto's print menu found under **File ➤ Print** in the menu bar, but then you'd have to assemble and bind the book, calendar, or cards yourself. It's just much easier (and truthfully, prettier) to let Apple do all the printing for you.

To buy your keepsake, follow these steps:

1. Make sure you have completed creating your book, card, or calendar to your liking, and then click the **Buy Book**, **Buy Card**, or **Buy Calendar** button at the bottom of your project's window.

2. A summary window is displayed showing what you are ordering and the price of it. You can enter the quantity you want to purchase and choose your shipping zip code and method. Once you have made your selections, click the **Check Out** button.

3. On the next screen, you'll need to enter your Apple ID. If you have an iTunes account, you have an Apple ID. If not, you can simply create one on this screen and then enter your credit card information.

Creating a Slideshow

Slideshows are great and, unlike other keepsakes, a free way to show off your photos. With a slideshow you can add text, music, and transitions quickly and easily to your photos and then show your pictures off with the click of a button.

To create a slideshow, follow these steps:

1. Select and album or event to create your show from; then click the **Create** button in iPhoto's toolbar, and choose **Slideshow** from the pop-up menu.

2. Your slideshow is automatically assembled and listed under the Slideshows header in iPhoto's source list. The slideshow window (Figure 8–22) allows you to browse through the photos in your slideshow one slide at a time. Here you can choose to preview your slideshow, play it, add effects, or export it.

Figure 8–22. *The slideshow window*

To browse through the photos in your slideshow, use the photo browser at the top of the screen. You can click and drag your photos around if you want to change the order they appear in your slideshow. Then, in the slideshow toolbar, you have the following options:

- **Preview button:** Quickly previews your slideshow in iPhoto's window. This is handy when you want to see how the show flows from a specific slide (like one in the middle).

- **Play button:** Plays your slideshow from the beginning in full screen.

- **Export button:** Opens the Export dialog box. This also allows you to save your slideshow as a movie, which is then playable on a number of devices including iPods, iPhones, and iPads.

- **Text Slide button:** Adds a text slide on top of a photo.

- **Themes button:** Shows you the slideshow themes chooser.

- **Music button:** Opens the music browser for your slideshow.

- **Settings button:** Opens the settings options for your slideshow.

To add text to your slideshows, follow these steps:

1. Click the Text slide button.

2. A text field appears over the photo that is displayed in the slideshow window (Figure 8–23). Enter any text you want.

Figure 8–23. *Entering text on a slide*

To choose a theme for your slideshow, follow these steps:

1. Click the **Themes** button in the slideshow toolbar.

2. A dialog box appears showing you the available themes (Figure 8–24). Move your mouse over the theme to preview it.

Figure 8–24. *Slideshow theme chooser*

3. When you have decided on a theme, click it so it is highlighted with a blue border.

4. Finally, click the **Choose** button. Your slideshow theme is then applied to your show.

To choose music for your slideshow, follow these steps:

1. Click the **Music** button in the slideshow toolbar.

2. A pop-up window appears that displays all your music settings (Figure 8–25). Basically, if you have music anywhere on your computer, it shows up in the Music Settings box.

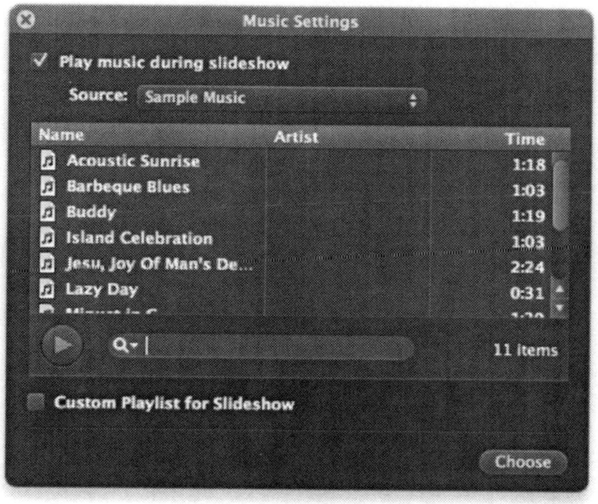

Figure 8–25. *Choosing your slideshow's music settings*

3. Choose the music source, such as iTunes, or even a specific playlist, and then choose a song from the list of available music.

4. If you want, you can preview the song by pressing the triangular **Play** button.

5. When you have decided on your song, click the **Choose** button to apply it.

To choose additional slideshow settings, follow these steps:

1. Click the **Settings** button in the slideshow toolbar.

2. A pop-up window appears displaying all the possible settings (Figure 8–26). These settings are broken down into two tabs: one for all slides and the other for just the selected slide.

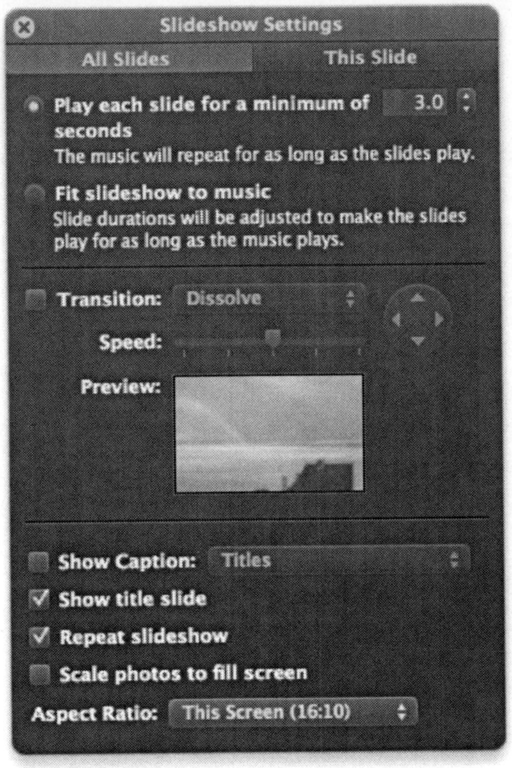

Figure 8–26. *Slideshow settings*

3. From these settings, you can choose the length of time each slide is displayed, the type of transitions between slides, the aspect ratio of the slideshow, and more. It's best just to play around with all the possible settings to see what you like best.

4. When you are done choosing your settings, simply close the Settings window, and your settings are applied.

To play a slideshow, follow these steps:

1. Click the Play button on the slideshow's toolbar (Figure 8–22). The slideshow will begin to play.

2. If you move your mouse while the slideshow is playing, on-screen controls appear (Figure 8–27).

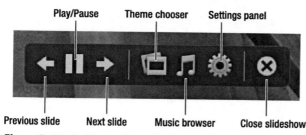

Figure 8–27. *A slideshow's on-screen controls*

3. The on-screen controls allow you to play or pause the slideshow, advance to the next slide or go back to the previous one, and quickly access and change the theme, music, and settings for the currently playing show.

Exporting Your Slideshow

Sometimes you might want to show your slideshow to someone but they aren't in the same room (or city) as your computer. Good news! They don't need to be. iPhoto allows you to export your slideshow to any iOS device, like an iPhone or iPad, and even lets you save it as a movie so you can e-mail it to people or post it to the Web. Keep in mind that some e-mail services may have a limit on the size of the movie that can be mailed.

To export your slideshow, follow these steps:

1. Click the **Export** button in the slideshow toolbar.

2. From the dialog box that appears (Figure 8–28), choose your export settings. If you are exporting the slideshow to display on a mobile device, the Mobile or Medium choice is fine. If you are exporting your show to display on a TV or the Web, the Large or Display option is a better bet.

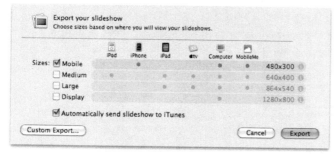

Figure 8–28. *Slideshow export options*

3. Check the box if you want your exported show to be automatically added to your iTunes library. Doing this ensures that it will sync with your iPhone the next time you connect it to your computer.

4.   When you are done choosing your export settings, click **Export**. Another dialog box appears asking you where on your computer you want to save the slideshow. Choose your location, and then click **OK**. The slideshow will take some time to export depending on its size.

5.   When the export is complete, you can use the resulting movie file any way you want—including uploading it to YouTube or e-mailing it to friends.

Creating an Instant Slideshow

Creating slideshows are cool, but with all the settings options, it can sometimes take a bit of work. If you just want to quickly play a selected event, album, or group of photos as a slideshow, you can create an *instant slideshow*, which lets you display your photos quickly and easily. An instant slideshow differs from a regular one in that it is never saved. So, if you create an instant slideshow, it will not show up in the Slideshows header in iPhoto's source list.

To create an instant slideshow, follow these steps:

1.   Choose the album, event, or group of photos you want to play as an instant slideshow.

2.   Click the **Slideshow** button at the bottom of the iPhoto toolbar (Figure 8–29).

Figure 8–29. *The slideshow button can be found at the bottom of most iPhoto windows.*

3.   The screen fades, and the first image from your selected photos appears. Over the image is a combined settings window (Figure 8–30). This combined settings window lets you quickly choose your slideshow theme, music, and additional settings, such as transitions and slide duration.

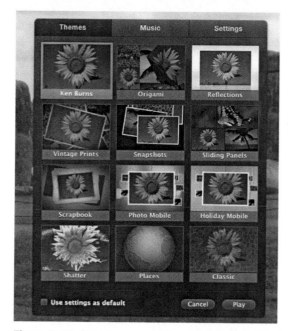

Figure 8–30. *Choosing your settings for an instant slideshow*

4. When you have made your settings, click the **Play** button, and your slideshow begins playing.

5. You can also check the **Use settings as default** check box if you want to immediately begin playing future instant slideshows with your current settings.

Summary

This chapter was a brief overview exploring the ways you can use your photos to create lasting keepsakes. I say "brief" because, as you can now see, there are so many settings and options when creating books, cards, calendars, and slideshows that it is not farfetched to say that even using the same photos, two people could never duplicate the other's keepsake project *exactly* even if they had a million years to do so.

But now you understand the basics of how to create and customize your keepsakes. Like anything with photography, the more you do it, the better you get. This chapter was primarily about the physical ways to share your photos. In the next chapter, I'll discuss the digital ways you can share your photos including via Facebook, Flickr, and e-mail.

Chapter 9

Sharing Your Photos Digitally

In the previous chapter, I talked about how you can use your photographs to create physical keepsakes such as books, cards, and calendars to share your photos with your family and friends. In this chapter, you'll explore all of the digital ways to share your photos. You'll learn how to easily upload your pictures from iPhoto to Facebook, Flickr, and MobileMe. You'll also learn how to export your photos to iWeb and iDVD.

I'll also discuss ordering professionally made prints of your photographs in the chapter for completeness sake, because it's grouped in the menu that allows you to share your photos digitally, the Share menu.

The Share Menu

As you can see in Figure 9–1, the Share button lies in the right corner in iPhoto's toolbar. The icon looks like a box with an arrow bursting out of it. Clicking the button displays the Share menu, which contains five options. These include ordering physical prints of your photos; uploading your photos to your MobileMe Gallery, Flickr account, or Facebook account; and lastly, e-mailing your photographs.

Figure 9–1. *The Share menu*

Ordering Prints

Remember the days when you would take photos with a film camera and then go to your local drugstore to have them printed? It was kind of expensive, somewhat of a pain, and, unless you went to the more expensive one-hour photo places, a long wait before you had nice glossy prints of your photographs.

Nowadays, the traditional print is being usurped by photo sharing sites such as Flickr, digital picture frames, and smartphones. However, sometimes it's still nice to have a printed photograph. You can of course print your own photos from within iPhoto using the File ▸ Print command in iPhoto's menu bar, but that's handy only if you have a really good photo printer.

Sometimes it's nice to send professional-quality prints to people who still like physical copies, such as grandparents. With this in mind, Apple has given iPhoto users a way to order physical prints of photos in their iPhoto Library and send them to anyone, anywhere in the world. Here's how:

1. Select one or more photos from your iPhoto Library.

2. Click the **Share** button in iPhoto's toolbar, and then click **Order Prints**.

3. In the Order Prints window that appears (Figure 9–2), select the size of each print and the number of copies of each print that you want. For one photo, you can order prints of multiple sizes. As you enter the size and number of prints, the subtotaled cost updates at the bottom of the screen.

4. (Optional) If you know you want the same size and number of copies for all your selected photos, use the **Quick Order** drop-down menu at the upper right of the order screen to choose the size, and then choose the number of copies using the up or down arrow.

Figure 9–2. *The Order Prints window*

5. Click the **Buy Now** button when you are done choosing your print sizes and copies.

6. On the Your Order screen that appears, enter a shipping zip code, and choose a shipping method.

7. Click the **Check Out** button.

8. On the next screen, you'll need to enter your Apple ID and click **Sign In**. If you have an iTunes account, you have an Apple ID. If not, you can create one on this screen.

9. Once you have signed in, the Confirm Order Details window appears. This is where you can enter the shipping address for the prints. When you are done, click the **Place Order** button.

10. Click **Done** to complete the order.

Sharing Your Photos Online

iPhoto's order prints feature is cool, but let's be honest, it's still a slow way to share your photos. After you order your prints, you still have to wait for them to arrive by mail. A much faster way to share your photos with friends and family is by doing so online.

Before you can share your photos using the built-in sharing tools in iPhoto, you need to make sure you have accounts with the three web sites iPhoto integrates with. Those web sites are MobileMe, Facebook, and Flickr.

For Facebook and Flickr, visit their web sites at www.facebook.com and www.flickr.com to sign up for a free account. If you want to use iPhoto with MobileMe sharing, however, you are going to have to purchase a MobileMe membership.

MobileMe is Apple's collection of online services including e-mail, contacts, calendars, online storage, and sharing services. Currently a MobileMe membership is $99 per year. You can find out more about MobileMe at www.apple.com/mobileme.

Setting Up Internet Accounts to Use in iPhoto

Once you have one or more of the online accounts needed for integrated iPhoto sharing, you'll need to make sure you have logged into those accounts through iPhoto. This enables you to perform publishing from within iPhoto directly to those accounts.

To set up Internet accounts in iPhoto, follow these steps:

1. Choose File ▸ Preferences from iPhoto's menu bar.

2. In the Preferences window that appears, click the **Accounts** button. The Accounts pane appears and displays any accounts you already have set up (Figure 9–3).

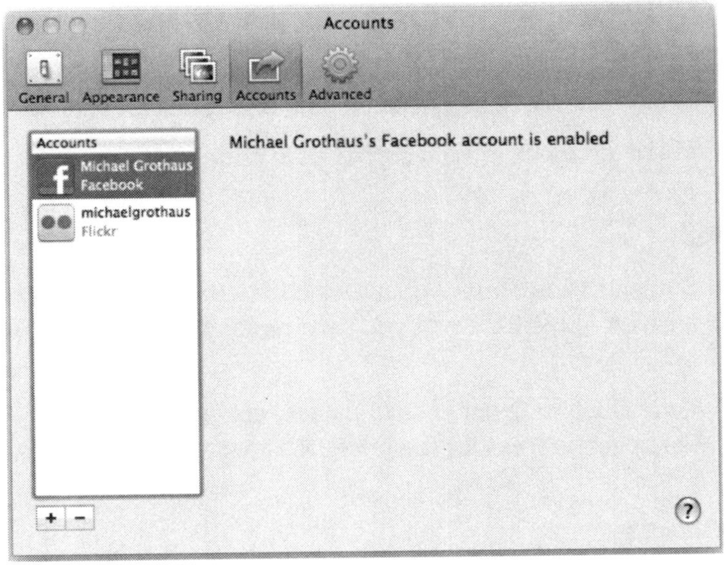

Figure 9–3. *iPhoto's Accounts pane*

3. In the Accounts pane, click the (+) button. A menu appears asking you to choose the type of account you want to add (Figure 9–4). Select one, and click Add.

Figure 9–4. *Choosing the account type you'd like to add*

4. A dialog box appears (Figure 9–5). Enter your account user name and password in it, and click **Log In**.

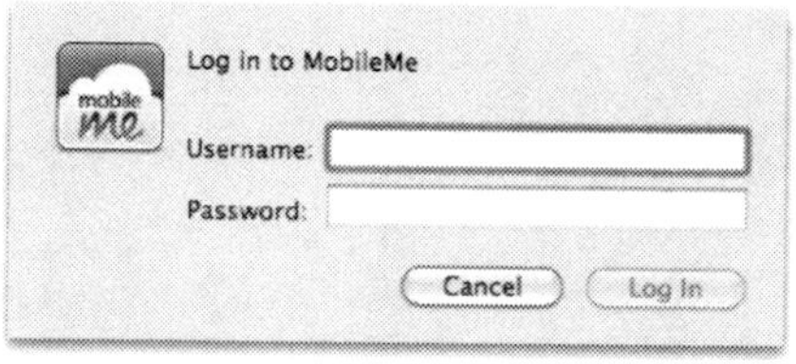

Figure 9–5. *Account login dialog box*

5. You user name and password are validated, and the account is added to the Accounts list.

Once you have enabled your accounts, they appear in iPhoto's source list under the Web header. You accounts are named after the name associated with the particular account. In Figure 9–6 you can see that the accounts are also identified with icons. The blue and white *f* symbolizes a Facebook account, the blue and pink dots are a Flickr account, and the white cloud and blue sky is a MobileMe account.

Figure 9–6. *Internet accounts show up in iPhoto's source list under the Web header.*

MobileMe

As I mentioned earlier, MobileMe is Apple's suite of online services. Some people love MobileMe; others think the $99 annual fee is a rip-off when there are other free services on the Web that provide the same things MobileMe does (for example, Gmail offers free e-mail, and Flickr offers free photo sharing). I like MobileMe a lot because it's so integrated into the entire Apple experience across your Macs and iOS devices such as iPhones and iPads. Again, you can decide for yourself whether MobileMe is right for you and find out more about MobileMe at www.apple.com/mobileme.

Publishing Photos to a MobileMe Gallery

To publish photos to a MobileMe gallery, follow these steps:

1. From your iPhoto Library, select the photo or photos you want to publish. You can also choose to publish an entire event or album. To do so, simply select the event by clicking it or choose the album by clicking it in iPhoto's source list.

2. Once you have selected your photos, album, or event, click the **Share** button in iPhoto's toolbar, and then choose **MobileMe Gallery** from the pop-up menu.

3. The Share menu expands to become the MobileMe Galleries menu you see in Figure 9–7. From this menu you can choose **New Album**, which creates a new album on your MobileMe gallery containing the photos you have selected, or you can click any of the other albums in your MobileMe gallery to add your currently selected photos to that album.

    If you want to add photos to an existing MobileMe gallery, click that gallery, and you'll get a confirmation that the photos were uploaded to it, and then you are done. However, if you are uploading your photos to a new album in your MobileMe gallery, click the **New Album** button and follow the rest of the steps.

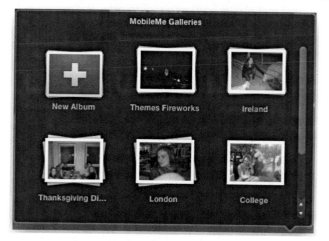

Figure 9–7. *The MobileMe Galleries menu*

4. After you have selected New Album, a dialog box appears with a host of MobileMe gallery settings for the new album you are creating (Figure 9–8).

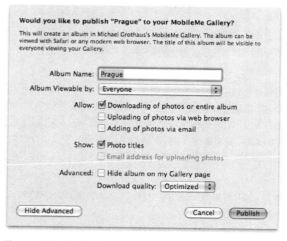

Figure 9–8. *MobileMe gallery publishing settings*

The settings are as follows:

- **Album Name:** This is the name of the album in your MobileMe gallery. By default, this is the name of the event of the iPhoto album you are uploading the photos from. You can change it to any name you want in the text box.

- **Album Viewable By:** This allows you to select who can view your album online. When set to Everyone, anyone with the web address of your album can view it. Only Me sets the album to private, and only you can view it online. Choosing Edit Names and Passwords displays another dialog box that lets you set up specific user names and passwords to give to your friends and family. Only people with the correct user names and passwords are able to view the web page with your photos.

- **Allow:** This selection has three options. You can check one, two, or all three.

  Downloading of photos or entire album: When selected, viewers of your gallery are able to download your photos to their computer.

  Uploading of photos via web browser: When selected, viewers of your gallery are able to upload their own photos to your MobileMe gallery.

  Adding of photos via e-mail: When selected, you or others are able to add photos to your gallery via e-mail.

- **Show:** When Photo titles is checked, the titles or file names of your photos are displayed in your gallery. When Email address for uploading photos is selected, an e-mail address is displayed that you or others can send photos to. Any photos sent to this e-mail are uploaded to your MobileMe gallery.

- **Advanced:** Hide album on my Gallery page hides your album on your MobileMe gallery page, but users can still access it if they know the direct web URL of the album.

- **Download Quality:** This allows you to set the quality of the photographs that people can download from your gallery. Choose Optimized for high-quality images that can be printed up to 16x20 inches. Choose Actual Size to let people download the photos at the same size as the original. Choosing Actual Size can mean longer download times.

5. Once you have chosen your publishing settings, click Publish. Your photos begin uploading to a new album in your MobileMe gallery.

Viewing Your MobileMe Galleries

Once you have published photos to your MobileMe galleries, you can view them on the Web or in iPhoto. Let's look at them in iPhoto first.

As you can see in Figure 9–9, you can select your MobileMe account in iPhoto's source list under the Web header. Your MobileMe Gallery is displayed in the body of iPhoto's window.

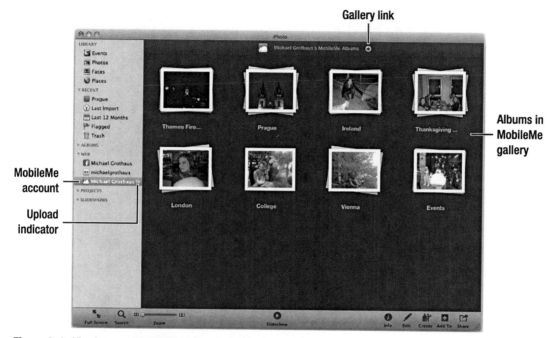

Figure 9–9. *Viewing your MobileMe gallery in iPhoto*

- **MobileMe account:** This is the name of your MobileMe account.

- **Upload indicator:** This is a swirling arrow that is shown when iPhoto is in the process of uploading photos to your MobileMe gallery.

- **Gallery link:** Clicking this arrow opens your web browser and takes you to the main MobileMe Gallery page.

- **Albums:** The main body of iPhoto's window shows you all the albums that your MobileMe gallery contains. iPhoto syncs with your MobileMe account to show you photos in your MobileMe galleries that have been uploaded outside of iPhoto. Although you can view these photos in iPhoto, they are not saved in your actual iPhoto Library. I'll talk about saving synced photos later.

Simply double-click any album in your gallery to view the contents of it. Figure 9–10 shows an individual MobileMe Gallery album when viewed in iPhoto.

Album link   Email link

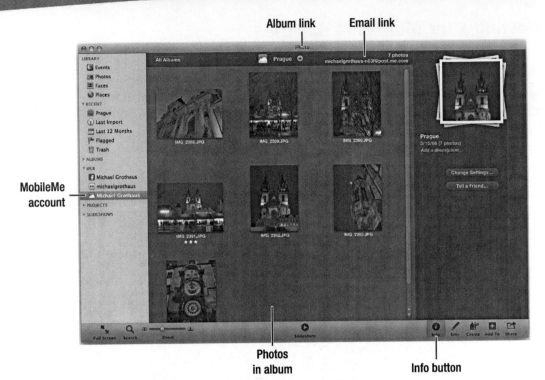

MobileMe
account

Photos
in album

Info button

Figure 9-10. *Viewing an individual album your MobileMe gallery in iPhoto*

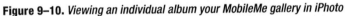

- **Album link:** Clicking this arrow launches your web browser and takes you to the specific album in your MobileMe gallery (Figure 9–11).

- **Email link:** This is the e-mail address you or others can use to send pictures to for uploading to the selected MobileMe gallery. This address appears only if you have selected to allow uploading via e-mail in the album's settings.

- **Change Settings:** Click this button in the Information pane to return to the MobileMe gallery publishing settings dialog box (Figure 9–8) to change the settings for the selected MobileMe gallery album.

- **Tell a Friend:** Click this button in the Information pane to send an e-mail to your friends with the web link and password to the album (if you've set one up).

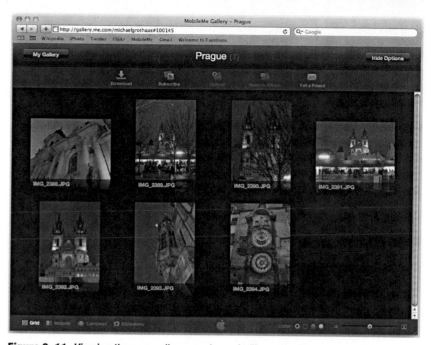

Figure 9–11. *Viewing the same album as shown in Figure 9–10 on your MobileMe Gallery on the Web*

Before I move on to the other sites you can publish your photos to through iPhoto, I want to touch on a couple of random notes about MobileMe galleries and iPhoto.

To delete photos from an album, follow these steps:

1. Choose your MobileMe account in iPhoto's source list.
2. Choose the album the photos are in.
3. Select the photo or photo you want to delete.
4. Press the Delete key on your keyboard.

The photos are removed from your online MobileMe gallery, but they still remain in your main iPhoto Library.

To delete a MobileMe Gallery album, follow these steps:

1. Choose your MobileMe account in iPhoto's source list.
2. Select the album you want to delete.
3. Press the Delete key on your keyboard.

The album is removed from your online MobileMe gallery; however, its photographs will still remain in your main iPhoto Library if that is where they originated. If others have uploaded photos to your online MobileMe gallery, see the following steps.

Saving Photos Added by Others

As I've talked about, you can allow others to upload photos to your online MobileMe galleries. When someone uploads a photo (via a web browser or via e-mail), the next time you open iPhoto, your MobileMe galleries will sync in iPhoto and display any photos your friends have uploaded.

However, these synced photos have not been saved to your iPhoto Library, and if you choose to delete the photos or album from your MobileMe gallery, any photos your friends have uploaded to your account will be deleted as well. So, before you delete a MobileMe album or photo through iPhoto, make sure you've saved any photos your friends have uploaded first. To do this, follow these steps:

1. Choose your MobileMe account in iPhoto's source list.

2. Choose the album the photos are in.

3. Select the photo or photo you want to save.

4. Drag that photo or photos to your Photos or Events header in iPhoto's source list. This will add them to your iPhoto Library, so even if you delete them from your MobileMe Gallery, you will now still have them saved on your computer.

Flickr

Flickr has been a popular image hosting site since its launch in 2004. Matter of fact, the site grew so much in popularity, Internet giant Yahoo! decided to buy it in 2005. If you're a current Flickr member, you'll be happy that Apple has built-in Flickr support in iPhoto. If you're not a member yet, you can go to www.flickr.com and create a free account.

You can also open a Flickr Pro account for an annual fee of $24.99. The Pro account gives you unlimited uploads, unlimited storage space, ad-free browsing and sharing, and more. Go to www.flickr.com/upgrade to read all about Flickr Pro accounts.

Publishing Photos to Flickr

To publish photos to Flickr, follow these steps:

1. From your iPhoto Library, select the photo or photos you want to publish. You can also choose to publish an entire event or album. To do so, simply select the event by clicking it, or choose the album by clicking it in iPhoto's source list.

2. Once you have selected your photos, album, or event, click the **Share** button in iPhoto's toolbar, and then choose **Flickr** from the pop-up menu.

3. The Share menu expands to become the Flickr Sets menu you see in Figure 9–12. From this menu you can choose **New Set**, which creates a new photo set on your Flickr page containing the photos you have selected. A *set* is just what Flickr calls an album.

    You can also click the Photostream button to add the selected photos right to your Flickr photostream. A *photostream* on Flickr is simply a collection of the latest photos you've uploaded.

    Click any of the existing Flickr sets to add your currently selected photos to that set.

Figure 9–12. *The Flickr Sets menu*

4. After you have selected to add your photos to a new set, the photostream, or an existing set, a dialog box appears with a few settings options for you to choose from (Figure 9–13).

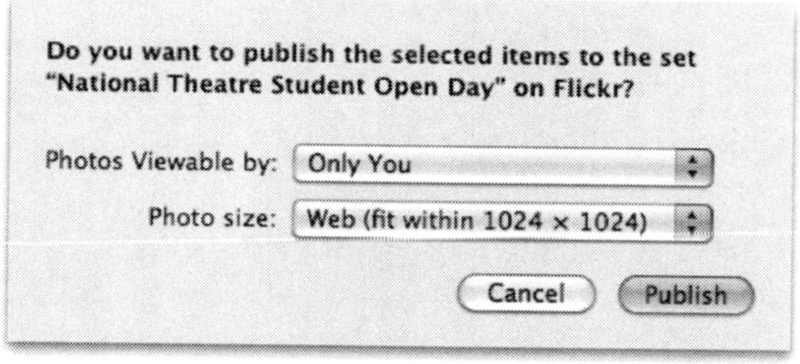

Figure 9–13. *Flickr upload settings*

■ **Photos Viewable By:** These are your photos' privacy settings. Choose who can view them, including you, your friends and family, or anyone.

- **Photo size:** This lets you set the size of your uploaded photos. You can choose from three options: web, half-size, or full-size. The last two options, half-size and full-size, are available only to Flickr Pro users.

5. Once you have chosen your publishing settings, click **Publish**. Your photos will begin uploading to your online Flickr account.

Viewing Your Flickr Sets

Once you have published photos to your Flickr account, you can view them on the Web or in iPhoto. Let's look at them in iPhoto first.

As you can see in Figure 9–14, you can select your Flickr account in iPhoto's source list under the Web header. Your Flickr sets are displayed in the body of iPhoto's window.

Figure 9–14. *Flickr Sets viewed in iPhoto*

- **Flickr account:** This is the name of your Flickr account.

- **Upload indicator:** This is a swirling arrow that is shown when iPhoto is in the process of uploading photos to your Flickr account.

- **Flickr Sets link:** Clicking this arrow opens your web browser and takes you to your Flickr Sets page.

- **Flickr Sets:** The main body of iPhoto's window shows you all the Sets that your Flickr account contains. If you click the Info button in the toolbar, you can see the Information pane displays very limited information for the selected set. This information includes the name of the set, the date it was taken, and how many photos the set contains. You can also enter a brief description of the set if you want.

  iPhoto syncs with your Flickr account to show you photos in your Flickr sets that have been uploaded outside of iPhoto. Although you can view these photos in iPhoto, they are not saved in your actual iPhoto Library. I'll talk about saving synced photos later.

Simply double-click any set to view the contents of it. Figure 9–15 shows an individual Flickr set when viewed in iPhoto.

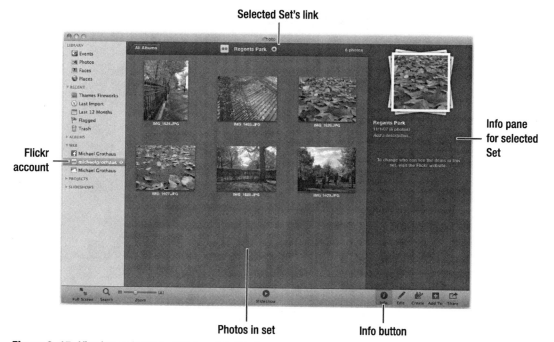

Figure 9–15. *Viewing an individual Flickr set in iPhoto*

- **Selected Set's link:** Clicking this arrow opens your web browser and takes you to the specific set in your Flickr account (Figure 9–16).

- **Info pane:** When no photo is selected, you'll see the same information displayed here as you did for the set in Figure 9–14. When you select a photo in the set, the Information pane shows you the standard photo information that iPhoto displays for any photo, such as EXIF data, the Places map, and Faces, Sharing, and Keywords information.

In Figure 9–16 you can see what your Flickr set looks like on the Web. You or others, if you give them permission, can upload photos to your Flickr sets via web browsers or e-mail. Any photos uploaded outside of iPhoto will be synced to your Flickr sets for viewing in iPhoto. However, they are not saved in your iPhoto Library unless you manually import them. I'll talk about this in a bit.

Figure 9–16. *Viewing the same set as shown in Figure 9–15 on your Flickr account on the Web*

Before you move on to the next site you can publish your photos to through iPhoto, I want to touch on a couple of random notes about Flickr sets and iPhoto.

To delete photos from a set, follow these steps:

1. Choose your Flickr account in iPhoto's source list.

2. Choose the sets the photos are in.

3. Select the photo or photos you want to delete.

4. Press the Delete key on your keyboard.

5. A dialog box appears asking you whether you are sure you want to remove the selected photo. Click **Remove Photo**.

6. Another dialog box appears warning you that the photo and associated comments will be removed from your Flickr account. Click Delete to confirm you want to remove the photo.

The photos are removed from your online Flickr account; however, if you uploaded them from your iPhoto Library, they still remain in your main iPhoto Library. Any photos synced from Flickr that have not been manually imported to your iPhoto Library will be moved to iPhoto's trash unless you choose to import them first (see the following steps).

To delete a Flickr Set, follow these steps:

1. Choose your Flickr account in iPhoto's source list.

2. Select the set you want to delete.

3. Press Command-Delete on your keyboard.

4. A dialog box appears asking whether you are sure you want to delete the set. Upon deletion, photos in the set will still exist in your online Flickr photostream unless you choose to delete the set and its photos. To only delete the set, click **Delete Set**. To delete the set and remove all photos from your Flickr photostream, click **Delete Set and Photos**.

5. Another dialog box appears asking you to confirm you want to delete the set and/or photos. Click **Delete Set** or **Delete Set and Photos** to confirm.

Depending on the option you choose, the set and/or its contents will be removed from your online Flickr account. Any photos downloaded from Flickr that have not been imported to your iPhoto Library are moved to iPhoto's trash unless you choose to import them first (see the following section).

Saving Photos Added by Others

As I briefly mentioned, Flickr allows you or others to add photos to your sets via the Web and e-mail. When someone uploads a photo to your Flickr account, the next time you open iPhoto, your Flickr sets sync in iPhoto and display any photos that have been added to your sets through sources other than iPhoto.

However, these photos have not been saved to your iPhoto Library, and if you choose to delete the photos or sets from your Flickr account, any photos uploaded to your account outside of iPhoto are deleted as well. Before you delete a Flickr set or photo through iPhoto, make sure you've saved any photos you want to keep that were not originally part of your iPhoto Library. To do this, follow these steps:

1. Choose your Flickr account in iPhoto's source list.

2. Choose the set the photos are in.

3. Select the photo or photo you want to save.

4. Drag that photo or photos to your Photos or Events header in iPhoto's source list. This adds them to your iPhoto Library, so even if you delete them from your Flickr account, you still have them saved on your computer.

Facebook

Unless you live under a rock, you've heard of Facebook. It's the wildly popular social networking site that has more than 600 million members and has spawned an Oscar-winning movie. Facebook lets you keep in touch with your friends, send messages, chat, play games, and, yes, upload and post photos. Matter of fact, the photo features on Facebook are the site's most popular function. In a single weekend, from New Years Eve to New Years Day 2011, 750 million photos were uploaded to Facebook (in *one* weekend!).

Of course, given Facebook's massive popularity, it's no surprise Apple has built-in Facebook photo sharing to iPhoto.

Publishing Photos to Facebook as Albums

To publish photos to Facebook as albums, follow these steps:

1. From your iPhoto Library, select the photo or photos you want to publish. You can also choose to publish an entire event or album. To do so, simply select the event by clicking it, or choose the album by clicking it in iPhoto's source list.

2. Once you have selected your photos, album, or event, click the Share button in iPhoto's toolbar, and then choose Facebook from the pop-up menu.

3. The Share menu expands to become the Facebook Albums menu you see in Figure 9–17. From this menu you can choose New Album, which creates a new album on your Facebook gallery containing the photos you have selected, or you can click any of the other albums in your Facebook gallery to add your currently selected photos to that album.

   If you are choosing to add photos to an existing Facebook album, click that album, and you'll get a confirmation that the photos were uploaded to it, and then you are done. However, if you are uploading your photos to a new album in your Facebook gallery, click the New Album button, and follow the rest of the steps.

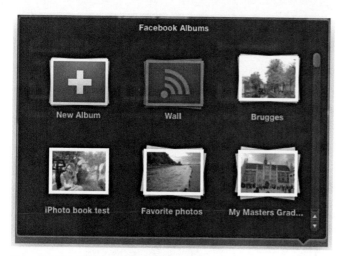

Figure 9–17. *The Facebook Albums menu*

4. After you have selected New Album, a dialog box appears with a few settings options for you to choose from (Figure 9–18).

Figure 9–18. *Facebook album settings*

- **Album Name:** This is the name of the album in your Facebook gallery. By default, this is the name of the event or iPhoto album you are uploading the photos from. You can change it to any name you want in the text box.

- **Photos Viewable by:** These are your photos' privacy settings. Choose who can view them, including everyone, friends of friends, or only friends.

5. Once you have chosen your publishing settings, click Publish. Your photos begin uploading to a new album in your Facebook gallery.

Viewing Your Facebook Albums

Once you have published photos to your Facebook gallery, you can view them on the Web or in iPhoto. Let's look at them in iPhoto first.

As you can see in Figure 9–19, you can select your Facebook account in iPhoto's source list under the Web header. Your Facebook gallery is displayed in the body of iPhoto's window.

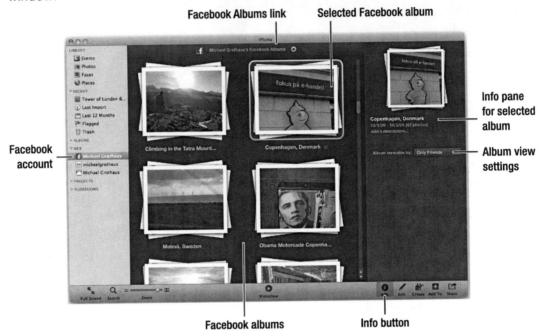

Figure 9–19. *Facebook albums viewed in iPhoto*

- **Facebook account:** This is the name of your Facebook account.

- **Facebook albums link:** Clicking this arrow opens your web browser and takes you to your Facebook albums page.

- **Facebook albums:** The main body of iPhoto's window shows you all the albums that your Facebook account contains. If you click the Info button in the toolbar, you can see the Information pane displays very limited information for the selected album. This information includes the name of the album, the dates its photos were taken, and how many photos the album contains. You can also enter a brief description of the album if you want.

    iPhoto syncs with your Facebook account to show you photos in your Facebook albums that have been uploaded outside of iPhoto. Although you can view these photos in iPhoto, they are not saved in your actual iPhoto Library. I'll talk about saving synced photos later.

- **Album View settings:** This drop-down menu lets you quickly change your album's privacy settings. Choose who can view them, including everyone, friends of friends, or only friends.

Simply double-click any album to view the contents of it. Figure 9–20 shows an individual Facebook album when viewed in iPhoto.

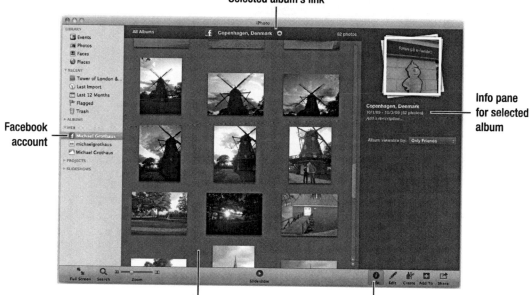

Figure 9–20. Viewing an individual Facebook album in iPhoto

- **Selected album's link:** Clicking this arrow opens your web browser and takes you to the specific album in your Facebook gallery (Figure 9–21).

- **Info pane:** When no photo is selected, you'll see the same information displayed here as you did for the set in Figure 9–19. When you select a photo in the set, the Information pane shows you the standard photo information that iPhoto displays for any photo, such as EXIF data, the Places map, and Faces, Sharing, and Keywords information.

In Figure 9–21 you can see what your Facebook album looks like on the Web. You can upload photos to your Facebook albums via web browsers. Any photos uploaded outside of iPhoto are downloaded to your Facebook albums in iPhoto. However, they will not be saved in your iPhoto Library unless you manually import them. I'll talk about this in a bit.

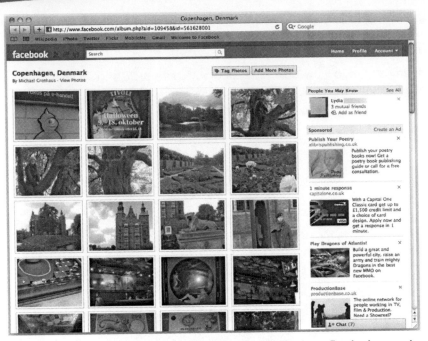

Figure 9–21. *Viewing the same set as shown in Figure 9–20 on your Facebook account on the Web*

Publishing a Photo to Your Facebook Wall

As any Facebook user knows, the primary feature of Facebook is the wall. Every user has a Facebook wall. It's where you can post status updates, links, and individual photos. iPhoto lets you quickly and easily post a single photo to your wall. Keep in mind that you can post only a single photo to your wall at a time. If you have multiple photos selected, you will not be able to select the **Wall** button (you can see in Figure 9–17 it's grayed out because I have selected multiple photos).

1. From your iPhoto Library, select the photo you want to post to your wall.

2. Once you have selected your photo, click the **Share** button in iPhoto's toolbar, and then choose **Facebook** from the pop-up menu.

3. The Share menu expands to become the Facebook Albums menu you see in Figure 9–22. Click the **Wall** button.

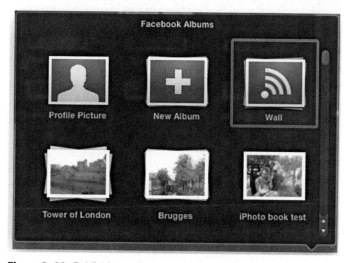

Figure 9–22. *Publishing a photo to your Facebook wall*

4. After you have selected Wall, a dialog box appears allowing you to add a comment about the photo (Figure 9–23). This comment will appear on your wall beneath the photo.

Figure 9–23. *Adding a comment to your wall photo*

5. Once you have added a comment, click the **Publish** button, and your photo and its comment are posted to your wall. Note that photos you have uploaded to your wall will not appear in your Facebook galleries in iPhoto.

As you can see in Figure 9–24, the uploaded photo has appeared on my Facebook wall. Note that it is shown that I uploaded the photo via iPhoto.

Michael Grothaus
Ah, Paris!

 32 seconds ago via iPhoto Uploader · 🔒 · Like · Comment · Share

Figure 9–24. *The uploaded photo on my Facebook wall*

Changing Your Facebook Profile Picture from Within iPhoto

Let's face it; social networking sites such as Facebook are very egocentric. And nothing screams ego more than the photo you use as your profile picture. You want to look good or, at the very least, make sure the picture you use to represent you says something about you (even if it's "I don't care what I look like!").

iPhoto allows you to change your Facebook profile within the iPhoto itself. Here's how:

1. From your iPhoto Library, select the photo you want to use as your profile picture. Make sure to edit and crop it to your liking before you upload it. This is where that Retouch button really comes in handy (see Chapter 7).

2. Once you have selected your photo, click the **Share** button in iPhoto's toolbar, and then choose **Facebook** from the pop-up menu.

3. The Share menu expands to become the Facebook Albums menu you see in Figure 9–25. Click the **Profile Picture** button. Note that you will see the Profile Picture button when you have only one photo selected. If you have more than one photo selected, the button is not displayed.

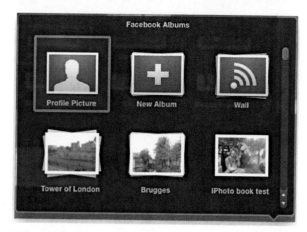

Figure 9–25. *Changing your Facebook profile picture in iPhoto*

4. After you have clicked Profile Picture, a dialog box appears asking whether you want to set the photo as your profile picture (Figure 9–26). Click Set, and you're done.

Figure 9–26. *No monkeying around. Make sure you've chosen the right profile picture.*

Facebook and iPhoto Odds and Ends

Before I continue discussing other ways you can share your photos digitally, let me mention of few important things regarding Facebook and iPhoto.

Faces Tagging

As mentioned in Chapter 5, iPhoto's facial recognition technology—Faces—lets you name and keep track of your friends and family in iPhoto. When you name a person in iPhoto and then upload that photo to Facebook, the person's Faces name is transformed into a Facebook tag. Tagging people in Facebook means you've marked a photo specifying who is in it. See Chapter 5 for more information on Faces naming and Facebook tagging.

Deleting Photos from a Facebook Album

To delete photos from a Facebook album, follow these steps:

1. Choose your Facebook account in iPhoto's source list.

2. Choose the album the photos are in.

3. Select the photo or photo you want to delete.

4. Press the Delete key on your keyboard.

5. A dialog box appears asking you whether you are sure you want to remove the selected photo. Click **Remove Photo**.

6. Another dialog box appears warning you that the photo and associated comments will be removed from your Facebook account. Click Delete to confirm you want to remove the photo.

The photos will be removed from your online Facebook account; however, if you uploaded them from your iPhoto Library, they will still remain in your main iPhoto Library. But any photos synced from Facebook that have not been manually imported to your iPhoto Library are moved to iPhoto's trash unless you choose to import them first (see the following steps).

Deleting Entire Facebook Albums

To delete entire Facebook albums, follow these steps:

1. Choose your Facebook account in iPhoto's source list.

2. Select the album you want to delete.

3. Press Command-Delete on your keyboard.

4. A dialog box appears asking you whether you are sure you want to delete the album. Click Delete, and your album is deleted from your online Facebook account.

Any photos synced from Facebook that have not been imported to your iPhoto Library are moved to iPhoto's trash unless you choose to import them first (see the following steps).

Saving Photos Added to Facebook Albums Outside of iPhoto

As I briefly mentioned, Facebook allows you to add photos to your account via the Web. When you externally upload a photo to your Facebook account, the next time you open iPhoto, your Facebook albums will sync in iPhoto and display any photos that have been added to your albums through sources other than iPhoto.

However, these photos have not been saved to your iPhoto Library, and if you choose to delete the photos or albums from your Facebook account, any photos uploaded to your account outside of iPhoto are deleted as well. So, before you delete a Facebook album or photo through iPhoto, make sure you've saved any photos that were not originally part of your iPhoto Library. To do this, follow these steps:

1. Choose your Facebook account in iPhoto's source list.

2. Choose the album the photos are in.

3. Select the photo or photo you want to save.

4. Drag that photo or photos to your Photos or Events header in iPhoto's source list. This adds them to your iPhoto Library, so even if you delete them from your Facebook account, they are still saved on your computer.

Sharing Photos via Email

It wasn't long ago that e-mail was the preferred way to share digital photos. Now however, with the rise of social networking sites, e-mail is quickly being usurped. Matter of fact, I just read the other day that e-mail usage dropped 32 percent in 2010, largely because of social network sites and texting. Maybe, however, people just need a cooler way to e-mail their photos. That's where iPhoto comes in.

Using iPhoto, you can create cool themes in the body of your e-mail to display your photos. These themes allow you to arrange your photos in interesting ways, kind of like if you were laying them out on a poster. You can then add and format your own text, change the layout of the photos, and more, all from within iPhoto!

At the time of this writing, iPhoto '11 offers ten e-mail themes including classic, journal, snapshots, corkboard, cardstock, announcement, celebration, collage, letterpress, and postcard. However, Apple frequently issues new, free updates to iPhoto (see Chapter 1), which may sometimes include new themes.

Before you can send photos from within iPhoto, you need to make sure you've entered your e-mail information. If you are already using Mac OS X's Mail app, iPhoto automatically imports your e-mail information and settings so you're ready to go. If you check your e-mail only in a web browser, however, you'll need to manually enter your e-mail settings in iPhoto.

To manually add your e-mail account to iPhoto, follow these steps:

1. Choose **File ▸ Preferences** from iPhoto's menu bar.

2. In the Preferences window that appears, click the **Accounts** button. The Accounts pane appears and displays any accounts you already have set up (Figure 9–3).

3. In the Accounts pane, click the (+) button. A menu appears asking you to choose the type of account you want to add (Figure 9–4). Select **Email**, and click **Add**.

4. A dialog box appears (Figure 9–27) asking you to choose your e-mail provider. Select it, and then click OK.

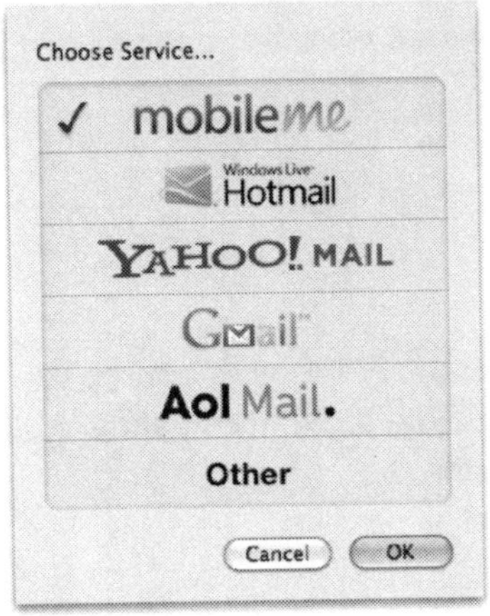

Figure 9–27. *Choosing your e-mail account*

5. An account dialog box appears (Figure 9–28). Enter your e-mail account information, and click OK. You user name and password will be validated, and the account will be added to the Accounts list.

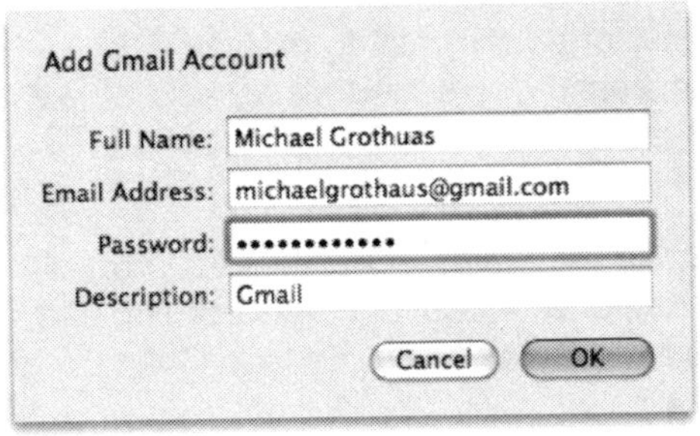

Figure 9–28. *Entering your e-mail account information*

Once you have set up your e-mail account, you are now ready to use iPhoto's built-in e-mail features. To e-mail your photos from within iPhoto, follow these steps:

1. Select the photos you want to e-mail. You can choose up to ten photos to e-mail in one message.

2. Once you have selected your photos, click the **Share** button in iPhoto's toolbar, and then choose **Email** from the pop-up menu. The e-mail composition window is displayed, as shown in Figure 9–29.

Email header

Theme
selector

Photo
settings

Body of email

Figure 9–29. *iPhoto's e-mail composition window*

3. In the composition window, choose the following settings:

- **Email header:** Enter the recipient's e-mail address and a subject for your e-mail.

- **Theme selector:** Choose which theme you want to display your photos in the body of the e-mail.

- **Photo settings:** Check Attach photos to message if you want to include downloadable versions of the photos you are sharing as a single attachment. This option allows your recipient to save the photos to their computer. Then use the Photo Size drop-down menu to choose the size of your photo attachments including optimized (which chooses the best size for e-mailing), small, medium, large, or original size.

If you choose not to include the photos as an attachment, the e-mail contains only what you see in the body of the message, effectively a single image of text and photos.

4. Once you have made these selections, go ahead and manipulate the body of the e-mail any way you like. Drag and drop photos to swap their positions; click a photo to zoom into it, and then drag it around to center on the part of the image you like. Click empty text fields to write your own messages, and then customize the text using the pop-up format menu.

5. When you are done editing the body of the e-mail, click the **Send** button, and your e-mail is sent.

Viewing Sharing Information for a Photo

iPhoto keeps an entire history for each photo you share. This history is stored under the Sharing header in a photo's Information pane. To view the sharing history, select the photo, click the Info button in the toolbar, and in the Information pane click the Sharing header so its contents are expanded.

As you can see in Figure 9–30, the Sharing header lists all the ways you've shared the selected photo and the dates and times you shared it. Information that shows up in the sharing header can show you any of the following:

- **E-mail status:** You can see who the photo was e-mailed to. Also, clicking the e-mail notification opens that e-mail again in iPhoto, which allows you to send the same e-mail again to different recipients.

- **Flickr status:** See whether you've uploaded the photo to Flickr. Click the Flickr notification to be taken to the photo in your web browser.

- **MobileMe status:** See whether you've uploaded the photo to your MobileMe Gallery. Click the MobileMe notification to be taken to the photo in your web browser.

- **Facebook status:** See whether you've uploaded the photo to Facebook. You can also see any Facebook comments on the photo under the Sharing header. Additionally, you can see any "likes" received on the photo. Click any of the Facebook notifications to be taken to the photo in your web browser.

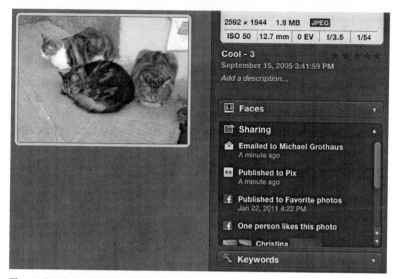

Figure 9–30. *A photo's sharing history*

Sending Your Photos to iWeb or iDVD

iWeb and iDVD are two of the other applications that make up the iLife suite. Apple allows you to easily send your photos from iPhoto right into a new or currently open iWeb site or iDVD project.

To send your photos to iWeb, follow these steps:

1. Select the photos, or an entire event or album of photos, that you want to send to iWeb.

2. From iPhoto's menu bar choose Share > Send to iWeb ▸ Photo Page. iWeb opens automatically, and the photos are applied to a new photo page on your iWeb site. You can also choose Share ▸ Send to iWeb ▸ Blog. iWeb opens automatically, and the photos are added to a new blog post on your iWeb site.

To send your photos to iDVD, follow these steps:

1. Select the photos, or an entire event or album of photos, that you want to send to iDVD.

2. From iPhoto's menu bar, choose Share ▸ iDVD. The selected photos are optimized for DVD viewing. iDVD launches automatically, and the photos are added as a new menu item.

Burning Photos to a CD or DVD for Viewing in iPhoto

With all the ways to share your photos digitally, CDs and DVDs are quickly showing their age. All physical media seems destined for the scrap heap as Internet connections become faster and ubiquitous. Still, iPhoto allows you to easily burn an iPhoto CD or DVD. The hang-up here, though, is that the photos on the disc you create using iPhoto can be viewed only using a Mac running the same version of iPhoto. Keep that in mind before you burn a DVD of your photos and mail it to your parents who are on a Windows PC.

To burn an iPhoto CD or DVD, follow these steps:

1. Select the photos or an entire event or album of photos you want to burn to a DVD or CD.

2. From iPhoto's menu bar, choose **Share ▸ Burn**.

3. A dialog box appears warning you the CD or DVD about to be created will be viewable only in iPhoto. Click OK.

4. Insert a blank CD or DVD disc into your Mac's optical drive. The disc's information appears at the bottom of the iPhoto window (Figure 9–31). Enter a name for the disc in the field provided.

Figure 9–31. *Burning your photos to a disc*

5. Click the **Burn** button.

6. A burn disc window appears. Click the **Burn** button again to begin burning your disc. Depending on how many photos you are burning to your disc, the burn may take a long time.

> **NOTE:** You *can* burn your photos to a CD or DVD on your Mac and then give the disc to your friends who have Windows PCs. However, you'll have to do it outside of iPhoto. The easiest way to do this is create a folder on your desktop and drag any photos you want to burn into it. Select the folder on your desktop, and from the Finder's menu bar, choose **File > Burn [name of folder] to Disc**.

Setting a Photo as Your Desktop Picture

Sometimes it's just cool to display your favorite photo as your desktop picture. Apple has made it easy to do this right from within iPhoto. To set an iPhoto picture as your desktop picture, follow these steps:

1. Select the photo you want to use as your desktop picture.

2. From iPhoto's menu bar choose **Share ▸ Set Desktop**. The selected photo appears as your desktop picture.

You can also use multiple photos as your desktop picture. If you select multiple photos and then choose **Share ▸ Set Desktop** from iPhoto's menu bar, the first photo selected is set as the desktop picture, and after a period of time, the desktop picture automatically changes to the next photo in the sequence. You can adjust the length of time it takes for this to happen in your Mac's System Preferences. Choose **⌘ ▸ System Preferences** from the menu bar, and then click **Desktop & Screen Saver**. Choose the Screen Saver tab, and select the length of time to change the desktop picture from the **Change Picture** drop-down menu.

Summary

As you can now see, there's no shortage of ways to share your photos digitally in iPhoto. Whether it's by e-mail, social networks, or DVD, iPhoto lets you share your memories quickly and easily. Now that you know all the ways iPhoto helps you digitally share your photos, the next time someone asks you to send them a picture, the only thing you'll need to know is in what medium they want to receive it.

Chapter 10

Advanced iPhoto Tips and Tricks

In this chapter, I'm going to tell you about a random assortment of settings, hints, tips, and tricks that you can use to make your iPhoto experience even better. These include tips for using iPhoto in Full Screen mode, playing and editing videos in iPhoto, handling your iPhoto Library file, backing up your iPhoto Library, and more.

Full-Screen View

Previously iPhoto had a Full Screen mode available only when editing photos, but with iPhoto '11 Apple brought full-screen to the entire app. Now no matter what you are doing—whether it's creating an event, editing a photo, or making keepsakes—you can do it using every single pixel on your screen. That's the primary benefit of using Full Screen mode—using every millimeter of your gorgeous Apple display to navigate, organize, share, and edit your photos.

To enter Full Screen mode, do one of the following:

- Click the **Full Screen** button in iPhoto's toolbar (Figure 10–1).
- Choose **View ➤ Full Screen** from iPhoto's menu bar.

Figure 10–1. *The Full Screen view button*

When you enter Full Screen mode, your entire desktop is replaced with iPhoto. As you can see in Figure 10–2, iPhoto in Full Screen mode has a different layout than it does in regular view. Events, for example, are arranged the same, but you no longer have a source list on the left side of the application; instead, all your Events, Faces, Places,

Albums, and Projects sections have been moved to the toolbar at the bottom of the screen.

Figure 10–2. *Events in Full Screen mode*

It's important to note that with the exception of the rearranged toolbar at the bottom of the screen, iPhoto works in Full Screen mode exactly as it does in regular view.

The Full-Screen Toolbar

iPhoto's full-screen toolbar is at the bottom of the Full Screen mode. For the most part, it's the same toolbar in iPhoto's regular view, with the exception of the source buttons (Figure 10–3).

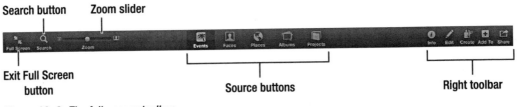

Figure 10–3. *The full-screen toolbar*

- **Full Screen:** Click this button to exit Full Screen mode.

- **Search:** Click this button to perform a search.

- **Zoom:** Adjust this slider to zoom into or out of photos or adjust the size of thumbnails and events.

- **Source buttons:** Instead of a source list, you have the source buttons. These include Events, Faces, Places, Albums, and Projects. Click any of the buttons to view their respective sections.

- **Right toolbar:** This toolbar has the same buttons and functions as it does in regular view. Click the Info button to show the Information pane, click the Edit button to enter edit mode, click the Create or Add To button to make or add to keepsakes, and click the Share button to share your photos.

> **NOTE:** While in Full Screen mode, iPhoto's menu bar is hidden from view. To see it and access all the menu commands, simply move your mouse to the top of the screen. After a slight pause, iPhoto's menu bar appears.

Viewing Your Photos Full-Screen

Just like in regular view, when you double-click an event in Full Screen mode, all the photos in the event are displayed. Likewise, when you double-click a photo in Full Screen mode, the photo is displayed just as it was in regular view (Figure 10–4).

Figure 10–4. *Editing an individual photo in Full Screen mode*

Likewise, Figure 10–5 shows you what Faces looks like in Full Screen mode, and Figure 10–6 shows you what Places looks like. Not much difference at all.

Figure 10–5. *Faces in Full Screen mode*

Figure 10–6. *Places in Full Screen mode*

Viewing Albums and Projects Full-Screen

As mentioned, because you don't have a source list in Full Screen mode, all the source list sections (Events, Faces, and Places) are shown as buttons in Full Screen mode's toolbar. You'll notice that there are two buttons that were previously headers in iPhoto's source list: Albums and Projects.

Albums

Figure 10–7 shows you the Albums section in Full Screen mode. It combines three headers from the source list: Albums, Sharing, and Slideshows. When you click the Albums button, you'll see all your albums displayed as thumbnails, with the first photograph in the album being used to represent the entire album.

Figure 10–7. *Viewing your albums in Full Screen mode*

At the top of the Albums screen you'll find all your regular and smart albums. Below those, if you have any Facebook, Flickr, or MobileMe galleries set up, you'll find headings for the albums and sets in those galleries. Below any shared galleries, you'll find any slideshows you've created. Double-click any album to view its contents, or double-click a slideshow to play it.

Projects

When it comes to viewing your project in full-screen, Apple decided to make its presentation and organization visually appealing. Apple did this by creating a "project shelf" that nicely displays all your books, calendars, and cards on a virtual shelf. When you click the Projects button in Full Screen mode, the project shelf appears (Figure 10–8).

Figure 10–8. *The project shelf in Full Screen mode*

As you can see, the project shelf contains all the keepsakes you have selected. When you click a keepsake, a spotlight shines down on it from overhead. To view and edit the contents of a keepsake, double-click it, and you'll be taken to the project's layout screen.

Playing and Editing Video

Today the average digital still camera also records video. When you import your photos into iPhoto, any videos you have recorded on the camera are imported as well. The videos are placed in the same event as the photos they were imported with. You can easily distinguish between a photo and video in iPhoto's library just by looking at its thumbnail. As you can see in Figure 10–9, a small opaque bar runs along the bottom of a video clip. The bar shows you a camera icon, signifying that the thumbnail is a video, and it also shows you the total length of the video in minutes and seconds.

Figure 10–9. *A video clip's thumbnail icon in iPhoto*

To play a video in your iPhoto Library, do this:

■ Double-click the video's thumbnail. The video expands to fill iPhoto's window and begins playing.

As you can see in Figure 10–10, a menu appears over the video that allows you to control its playback, including adjusting the clip's volume levels, playing it, pausing it, fast-forward or rewinding it, and scrubbing through it using the clip's slider at the bottom of the control menu.

Volume   Rewind, Play/Pause,   Action menu
          and Forward buttons

Figure 10–10. *Controlling a video's playback and settings*

You'll also notice a small cog icon to the left of the control menu. Apple calls this the *Action menu*, and clicking it opens a small pop-up menu with additional actions for your video clip:

- **Actual Size:** This plays the clip in iPhoto's window in its actual size (resolution). Selecting this could display your clip smaller on your screen because, generally, Mac screens have a higher resolution than even HD video.

- **Fit to Window:** Selecting this plays the clip at the same size as iPhoto's window.

- **Trim:** Selecting this enters trim mode. Trim mode allows you to clip off the edges of your video so you can save just the portion you want. iPhoto's trim feature isn't a full-on video editor and is in no way comparable to iMovie—Apple's video-editing software that is also part of the iLife suite. However, trim mode is handy for fine-tuning your video clips. When you record video clips with your still camera, it's usually just to capture a quick clip of something, and many times you begin recording seconds before you come to the "meat" of the video and continue recording for seconds after. The Trim function allows you to cut off this excess baggage.

To trim a video clip, follow these steps:

1. Double-click the video in iPhoto so it appears in iPhoto's window.

2. Click the **Action** button in the control menu.

3. Select **Trim** from the pop-up menu that appears. The yellow trim controls appear (Figure 10–11).

Figure 10–11. *The trim controls*

4. Click and drag either or both ends of the yellow trim handles toward the center. Dragging the ends shortens the clip by trimming excess material at the beginning and end.

5. When you have trimmed the ends of your clip to your liking, click the **Trim** button. Any part of the video to the left or right of the trim handles is excised from the video. If you change your mind about the edit, you can always undo it by selecting the **Action** pop-up menu and choosing **Reset Trim**.

TIP: To quickly group all of your imported video clips together in one location, create a smart album for your video clips. From iPhoto's menu bar, choose **File ➤ New ➤ Smart Album**; then in the smart album dialog box that appears, set your conditions to Photo "is" Movie. A new smart album is created with all the video clips in your iPhoto Library.

iPhoto Preferences

iPhoto, like most other Mac applications, has a selection of preferences that can be changed in order to optimize your own personal user experience. These preferences can be accessed from iPhoto's menu bar by choosing **iPhoto ➤ Preferences**. At the top of the preferences window that appears is a series of five tabs: General, Appearance, Sharing, Accounts, and Advanced.

General Preferences

The General preferences are just that—general iPhoto settings that you can adjust to your liking. You can see the general preferences in Figure 10–12.

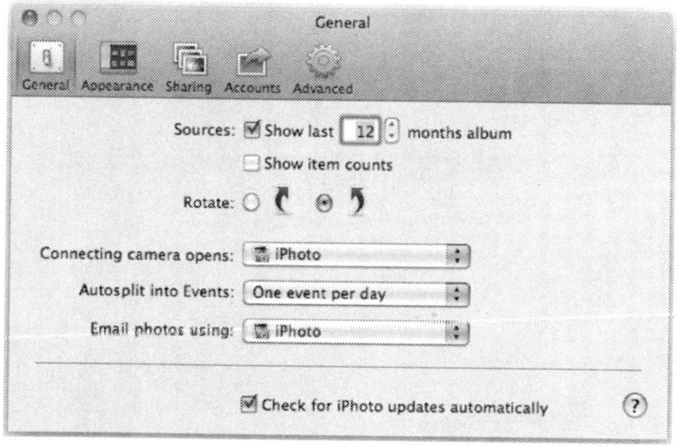

Figure 10–12. *The General preferences*

- **Show last "12" months album:** When this is selected, iPhoto will display the Last "12" Months album in its source list. Uncheck this box, and the Last "12" Months album will not appear. You can also set the number of months you want the last month album to span.

- **Show Item Counts:** When this is checked, the total numbers of photos and events are shown in parentheses next to their respective categories (Photos and Events) in the source list. Additionally, when Show Item Counts is checked, the number of photos an album contains is shown in parentheses next to the album's name.

- **Rotate:** Select which way you want the Rotate button to rotate your photos—clockwise or counterclockwise.

- **Connecting camera opens:** From the drop-down menu choose what you want to happen when you connect your camera to your Mac. By default, iPhoto opens automatically. You can change this to set other photo apps to open automatically when you connect your camera, or you can set this to No application; you'll need to manually launch iPhoto after your camera is connected if you want to import photos from it.

- **Autosplit into Events:** This drop-down menu lets you split imported photos into events by the day or week or into two- or eight-hour gaps.

- **Email Photos using:** This drop-down menu lets you set the e-mail client you want to use when selecting the Email command from the Share menu. By default this is set to iPhoto. If you change it to another e-mail client, such as Outlook or Apple's Mail, you will not be able to use iPhoto's built-in e-mail themes when sending your photographs.

- **Check for iPhoto updates automatically:** When this is checked, iPhoto automatically checks to see whether there are any updates for the app and notifies you when an update is available for download.

Appearance Preferences

The Appearance preferences (Figure 10–13) let you change the appearance of iPhoto's main viewing area.

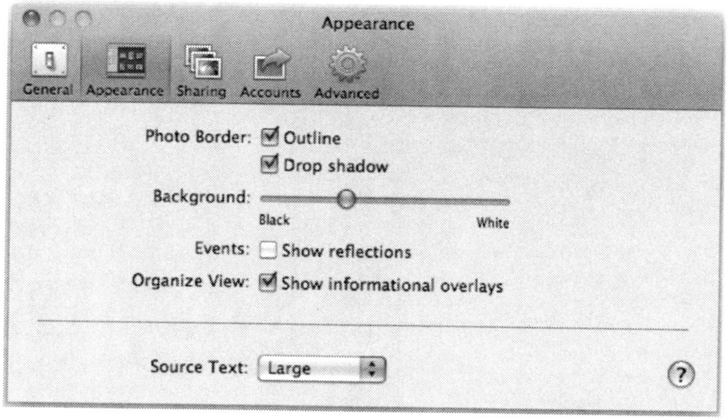

Figure 10–13. *Appearance preferences*

- **Outline:** When this is checked, your photos are displayed with a 1-pixel thick frame around them.

- **Drop shadow:** When this is checked, your photos are displayed with a subtle drop shadow around them.

- **Background:** Adjust this slider to change the background color of iPhoto's window.

- **Show reflections:** This is purely eye candy and, when checked, causes a reflection of an event's icon to show beneath the event.

- **Show informational overlays:** Informational overlays are the black bezel notifications that show the date, title, or ratings over your photos as you scroll through them in Events or Photos view.

- **Source Text:** This drop-down menu lets you choose a large or small font to use for the items in your source list. Choosing the small font is handy if you have dozens of albums in your source list because it lets you see more of the items in your source list at once.

Sharing Preferences

iPhoto allows you to share your photos over a local network with up to five computers. You can also set iPhoto to look for shared photos on your local network. iPhoto users who are viewing shared local photos can then drag the photos from a shared photo library into their iPhoto Library. Shared libraries show up in iPhoto's source list. You enable library sharing from the Sharing preferences (Figure 10–14).

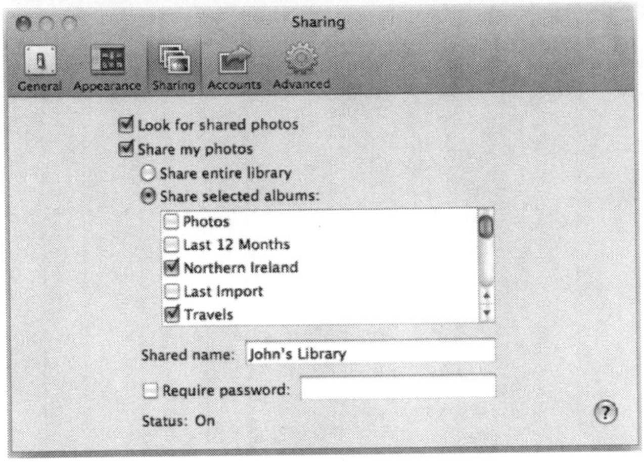

Figure 10–14: *The Sharing preferences*

- **Look for shared photos:** When this is checked, iPhoto looks for other shared iPhoto libraries on your local network. Any shared libraries show up in your iPhoto source list.

- **Share my photos:** When this is checked, you are enabling sharing of your iPhoto Library. You can choose between sharing the entire library or just sharing selected albums.

- **Shared name:** This is the name of your shared library that is displayed to other computers on your local network.

- **Require password:** If you want, you can require that others know and need to enter a password to view your shared library. Set the password by entering it in the text field.

Accounts Preferences

The Accounts preferences tab contains all the settings for online web sharing and e-mailing. Please refer to Chapter 9 where these settings are discussed in detail.

Advanced Preferences

The Advanced preferences (Figure 10–15) are those that most users won't need to adjust. However, if you want to be an iPhoto power user, it's important to know what they do.

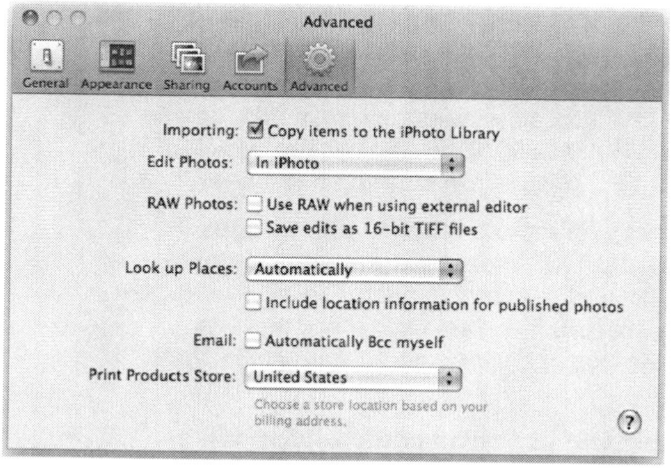

Figure 10–15. *iPhoto's advanced preferences*

- **Copy items to the iPhoto Library:** By default, when you import photos on your hard drive to your iPhoto Library, iPhoto makes a copy of the photos in your iPhoto Library. The original photos remain in their current location on your hard drive. If you uncheck this option, iPhoto creates reference files in your iPhoto Library that point to the actual files located elsewhere on your hard drive. I recommend you leave this option checked, unless you are severely low on disk space.

- **Edit Photos:** This allows you to choose which application the selected photo in iPhoto opens in when you click the Edit button in the toolbar. By default, the photo will open in iPhoto's editor. You can, however, select "In application" from the drop-down menu and then choose another photo editor on your Mac (such as Photoshop or Pixelmator).

  Although individual reasons will vary, some people like using an external photo editor if they are going to make advanced edits to photos that iPhoto cannot handle. For example, iPhoto does not allow you to use layers while editing your photographs. If you want to add layers to your photos, it is best to open them in Photoshop or Pixelmator.

- **Use RAW when using external editor:** If you select to open your photos in an external editor, checking this option causes the RAW version of the photo to open in the external editor. A RAW copy of a photo is the full, uncompressed digital bits of the photograph recorded by your camera's sensors. It is the purest-quality digital file you can have. However, unless you have a super-human eye or are using your photos in very large print campaigns, you won't need to use RAW files. Also, not all digital cameras capture photos in RAW format.

- **Save edits as 16-bit TIFF files:** If you edit RAW files within iPhoto, they are saved using a compression format known as JPEG. A JPEG file is good enough for high-quality prints, but you do lose some bits of data in the compression. TIFF is lossless compression, so you save on file size but still get almost RAW quality. Checking this box saves all your iPhoto edits as 16-bit TIFF files instead of JPEG files.

- **Look up Places:** When this is set to Automatically, iPhoto reads the location data in a photograph's EXIF information and goes out onto the Internet to fetch an exact address for that photo. This is how those photos appear on the Places map. If you set this setting to Never, iPhoto will not automatically look up your photograph's location data addresses or names.

- **Include location information for published photos:** If this box is checked, when you share your photos digitally—via e-mail, Facebook, or MobileMe, for example—the location of the photos is also published with the photos.

- **Automatically Bcc myself:** In e-mail terminology, BCC stands for "blind carbon copy." Check this box to send yourself a copy of any e-mail you send from within iPhoto. The recipient of the e-mail will not know you have also sent yourself a copy.

- **Print Products Store:** By default, this location is chosen by iPhoto based on the billing address associated with your Apple ID account. If, for some reason, you move to another country, you can select that country in the drop-down list so iPhoto knows to place your keepsake project orders with that country's print store.

iPhoto Library Tips

As I mentioned in Chapter 2, iPhoto organizes all your imported photographs into a single file on your Mac. This file is named iPhoto Library and can be found in the *User Name* ➤ *Pictures* folder on your Mac (see Figure 10–16). This one file contains every photo, including the original imported copies and any subsequent edits, in a single place.

As I mentioned in Chapter 2, the advantage of this centralized iPhoto Library file on your computer is twofold:

- It allows you to easily back up your entire photo library by simply copying the iPhoto Library file to an external hard drive.

- It ensures that all the photos on your computer are in one easy-to-find place and eliminates clusters of folders of pictures from being scattered around your Mac.

Figure 10–16. *The iPhoto Library file*

Revealing Photos in the Finder

At first glance, the iPhoto Library file looks like it's just a single file, but in actuality it's made up of hundreds of folders and subfolders. To see all these folders, right-click the iPhoto Library file, and then choose **Show Package Contents** from the contextual menu. A Finder window opens and reveals the contents of the iPhoto Library file.

Inside you'll see dozens of folders and files (Figure 10–17). Some of these folders contain the original master photographs; some contain their edits. Others contain data files that record the way you have your photos organized—such as which albums and events they go into.

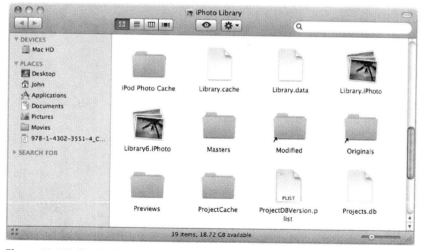

Figure 10–17. *The insides of the iPhoto Library file*

For whatever reason, you may want to locate one of iPhoto's photographs, whether it's the original master or an edited copy, in the Finder. Apple makes it easy to do this (meaning you don't have to select Show Package Contents in the iPhoto Library file and then dig through all its subfolders).

To locate the original or modified file of a photograph in the Finder, follow these steps:

1. Select the photograph in iPhoto.

2. From the iPhoto menu bar, select **File > Reveal in Finder** and then choose **Modified File** or **Original File** (Figure 10–18).

3. A Finder window opens showing you the location of the modified (edited) or original photograph.

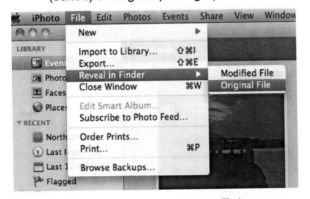

Figure 10–18. *Locating a photograph in the Finder*

Backing Up Your Photo Library

I cannot stress enough how important it is to regularly back up your iPhoto Library. I'm going to say it again—*you need to regularly back up your photo library*. The reasons are obvious: if your Mac is stolen and you have no external backup, all your photos are gone forever. Likewise, if the hard drive on your Mac becomes corrupted (unlikely, but as with any piece of hardware tech, it can happen), you'll lose all your photographs.

At first it might seem daunting to back up hundreds or even thousands of photographs, but that's where the beauty of iPhoto's single library file (Figure 10–16) comes in. Since it is just one file, you can simply drag and drop it to an external hard drive and wait for it to copy over. Once the copy is complete, every single photo, event, album, and keepsake in your iPhoto Library is backed up. How much easier could it get?

I suggest using an external hard drive as your backup device of choice for a few reasons: they are now relatively cheap, and you can use them for backing up other files on your Mac. In addition, chances are good that your iPhoto Library will eventually grow to such a size that it won't fit onto other forms of external media such as CDs, DVDs, and USB sticks.

If you hate the idea of manually backing up your iPhoto Library, Apple offers a wireless hard drive called Time Capsule. Time Capsule integrates with software in Mac OS X 10.6 called Time Machine that lets you set regular backup schedules and automatically backs up your files—including your iPhoto Library—whenever a change is made to them (even a single edit). You can also use the Time Machine software with any external hard drive, not just Apple's Time Capsule. You can learn more about Time Capsule and Time Machine at www.apple.com/timecapsule and www.apple.com/macosx/what-is-macosx/time-machine.html.

Creating Separate iPhoto Libraries

iPhoto allows you to create separate iPhoto Library files and then choose between which iPhoto Library file you want to load when you start iPhoto. At first, a separate iPhoto Library file for the same user might seem somewhat pointless, but if you are an ultra-organized type, you may want to have separate photo libraries for both your personal photos and your work photos. Most people won't be using separate iPhoto Libraries, but if you choose to, here's how you do it:

1. Quit iPhoto if you are currently in it.

2. Hold down the Option key on your keyboard, and then click the iPhoto icon in your Dock to launch iPhoto.

3. In the iPhoto Library selection window that appears (Figure 10–19), you'll see a list of all iPhoto Library files on your computer. Click the **Create New** button to create a new, empty iPhoto Library.

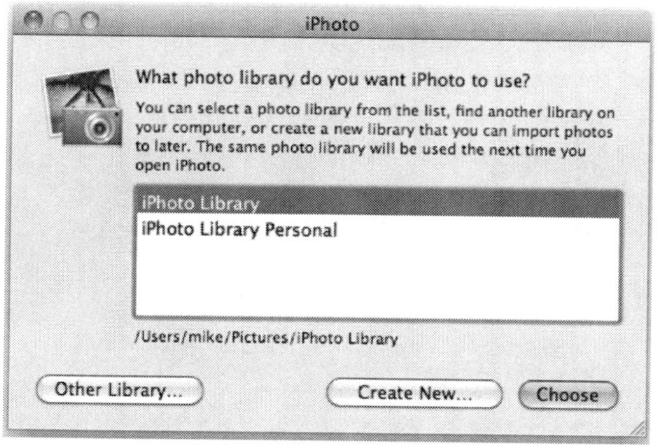

Figure 10–19. *The iPhoto Library selection window*

4. In the dialog box that appears, type a name for your new library, and choose a location to store the new photo library in. I recommend keeping all iPhoto Libraries in the Pictures folder, but you can place them anywhere you want.

5. Click the **Save** button. iPhoto opens the newly created library. The library will be empty and void of any pictures, albums, events, and projects until you import and create them.

Switching Between and Restoring iPhoto Libraries

By default, when you launch iPhoto, the last library it opened is the one that it opens again. However, you can switch between your various iPhoto Library files at any time by using the following steps. These steps are also the ones you follow to restore your iPhoto Library file on your Mac when you've copied it from an external hard drive backup.

1. Quit iPhoto if you are currently in it.

2. Hold down the Option key on your keyboard, and then click the iPhoto icon in your Dock to launch iPhoto.

3. In the iPhoto Library selection window that appears (Figure 10–19), you'll see a list of all iPhoto Library files on your computer that iPhoto has detected. If the iPhoto Library file you want to load is displayed, select it from the list, and click the Choose button. iPhoto loads the selected iPhoto Library.

    If the iPhoto Library you want to load is not displayed in the selection window, click the Other Library button. A Finder window appears that allows you to navigate to where your iPhoto Library file is located on your hard drive. Once you find it, select it, and click Open. iPhoto loads the selected iPhoto Library.

NOTE: Though you can load an iPhoto Library from an external hard drive, it is not wise to do so. Running large database files from an external drive can cause data instability, which can lead to corruption—or complete loss—of your photos. It's best to move any iPhoto Library file from an external drive onto your Mac's hard drive and then launch it from there. By all means, leave a copy of the iPhoto Library on your external hard drive as a backup; just don't actively use it in iPhoto.

Subscribing to a Photo Feed

iPhoto isn't all about viewing, sharing, and editing only your photos. It's also got a cool built-in feature that lets you follow the latest photos from your friends. You can even see the latest photos from professional photographers you like right from within your iPhoto Library. This is accomplished by subscribing to photo feeds.

A photo feed is simply a web site URL that you "bookmark" inside iPhoto. Any photographs that appear on the web page with the URL on it appear in iPhoto. I'll tell you how to set this up and then show you what a photo feed looks like in iPhoto.

To subscribe to a photo feed in iPhoto, follow these steps:

1. Use a web browser (like Safari) to visit the web site of the photographer you want to follow.

2. Once you locate the page of the web site containing that photographer's photos, click the RSS button in your browser's toolbar, and select RSS feed if you are given multiple options (Figure 10–20).

Figure 10–20. *Selecting a photo RSS feed in your web browser (photographs ©José Farinha)*

3. The RSS feed is displayed in your browser. Copy the URL of the RSS feed.

4. From iPhoto's menu bar, choose File ➤ Subscribe to Photo Feed. In the dialog box that appears (Figure 10–21), paste the RSS address of the web site into the text field, and then click the Subscribe button.

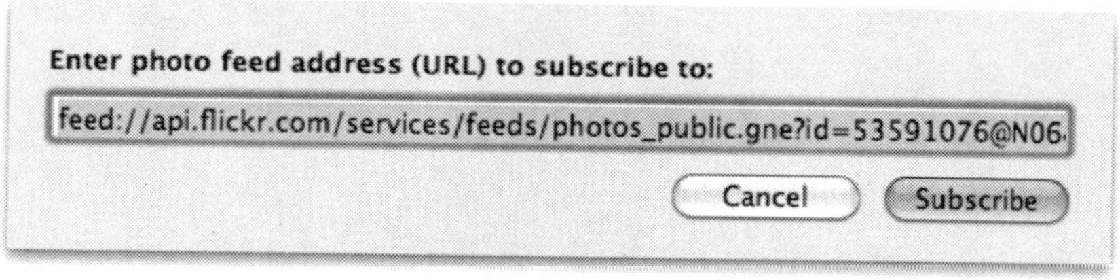

> **Enter photo feed address (URL) to subscribe to:**
>
> feed://api.flickr.com/services/feeds/photos_public.gne?id=53591076@N06
>
> Cancel   Subscribe

Figure 10–21. *Adding an RSS feed to iPhoto*

5. A new header titled Subscriptions appears in iPhoto's source list. Below it is the title of the feed you just subscribed to. When you select this feed, any photos associated with it are shown in iPhoto's window and downloaded to your library (Figure 10–22).

Figure 10–22. *Viewing a photo feed in iPhoto (photographs ©José Farinha)*

As you can see in Figure 10–22, I've subscribed to the feed of José Farinha, a popular Portuguese photographer. All his photos linked to that feed show up in my iPhoto Library. When he publishes new photos to his feed, iPhoto automatically downloads them the next time I open the application.

From my library, I can view the photos, share the feed photos via e-mail, or set them as my desktop picture. I cannot, however, use photos from a feed in any keepsake projects, nor can I edit them.

(I'd like to thank José Farinha for letting me use his photos in Figures 10–20 and 10–22 of this book. You can see more of his work at www.josefarinha.com.)

If you want to stop following a photo feed, you can simply unsubscribe from it. To do this, follow these steps:

1. Select the photo feed in iPhoto's source list.

2. Press the Delete key on your keyboard.

3. In the dialog box that appears, you'll be asked whether you want to delete the feed. You'll also be warned that the photos are not saved in your iPhoto Library and deleting the feed will move them to your trash. If you want to save the feed photos to your iPhoto Library, check the box that asks whether you would like to import the feed photos to your main iPhoto Library before deleting.

4. Click the Delete button to remove the feed.

Exporting Your Photos

As you've seen throughout this book, iPhoto offers users many ways to share their photos with others. These include creating physical keepsakes, such as books, calendars, and cards; creating slideshows; and sharing your photos on the Web.

However, sometimes you may want to use your photos in other applications or in other ways than iPhoto directly provides for. For example, you may want to create slideshow movies that could play on any device, or you may want to burn some photos onto a CD or DVD using applications other than iPhoto or iDVD.

iPhoto's export options are numerous, and they help you prepare your photo for use in an almost unlimited number of settings. Let's look at iPhoto's export options now. To export a photo, choose File ➤ Export from iPhoto's menu bar. In the export window that appears (Figure 10–23), you'll see four tabs that each provides a separate set of export setting based on what you'll be using your exported photos for. Let's go through all the export settings now.

File Export

The first tab in the export window is the File Export settings. These settings allow you to export a single photo or a group of photos as individual files, which you can then use in any way you want.

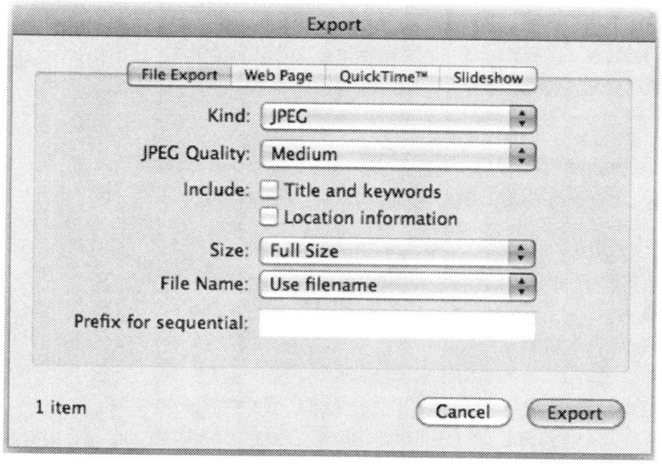

Figure 10–23. *Exporting photos as individual files*

To export photos as individual files, follow these steps:

1. Select the photo or photos in your iPhoto Library that you want to export.

2. Choose File ➤ Export from iPhoto's menu bar.

3. In the Export Photos window that appears (Figure 10–23), select the File Export tab.

4. You'll see a host of settings to choose from. Select the settings you want. The settings include the following:

  ▪ **Kind:** This is the type of file the photo will be exported as. You have five options from the drop-down menu.

    Original—Exports the master, unedited version of the photo that was originally imported into iPhoto.

    Current—Exports the photo as it currently is, edits and all.

    JPEG—This is the most common file format. If you are sharing the photo on the Web and don't plan to print it, JPEG is fine.

    TIFF—As mentioned earlier, TIFF is a lossless file format. It's a little better in quality than JPEG, but it also has a larger file size.

    PNG—This is another lossless file format. PNG files are a common file format for images you see on the Web.

  ▪ **JPEG Quality:** If you chose to export your file as a JPEG, you can set the JPEG quality in the pop-up menu here. Choose from low, medium, high, or maximum. Keep in mind the greater the quality, the larger the file size.

  ▪ **Include Title and Keywords:** When this is checked, any title or keywords associated with the photo are included in its EXIF metadata information.

  ▪ **Include Location Information:** When this is checked, any location data associated with the photo is included in its EXIF metadata information.

  ▪ **Size:** This drop-down menu lets you change the size, or resolution, of the photograph. Choose from small, medium, large, full size, or custom. Small and medium should be reserved for only web viewing. If you are going to print the photos, choose large (good for up to 4x6 prints), optimized (5x7 prints), or full size (8x10s or larger). You can also customize the export size by choosing Custom from the drop-down menu.

  ▪ **File Name:** This allows you to set the file name for the exported photo. Choose from using the photo's iPhoto title, using the photo's current file name, using the photo's album name followed by a sequential number, or simply using a sequential number for each exported file.

- **Prefix for sequential:** If you choose Sequential from the File Name menu, you can enter specific text to appear before each number in the sequence. So if you enter "Vacation" in the text box here, your exported photos will be named Vacation01, Vacation02, and so on.

5. After you have chosen your settings, click **Export**, and a Finder dialog box appears.

6. Choose where you want to save the exported files, and then click the **OK** button.

Web Page

The second tab in the Export window is Web Page (Figure 10–24). These settings allow you to export a group of photos as a simple web page that you can then upload to any server you have access to. This is just another way to put your photos on the Web and is for those of you who don't want to use iWeb to build a web site from scratch.

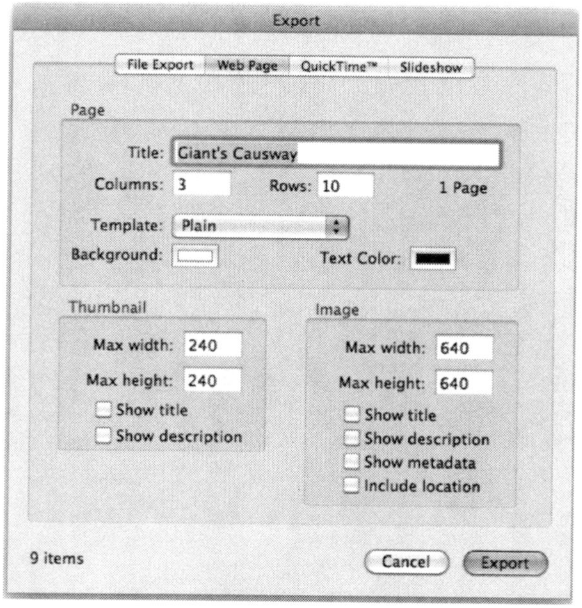

Figure 10–24. *Exporting your photos as a simple web page*

To export photos as a simple web page, follow these steps:

1. Select the photo or photos in your iPhoto Library that you want to export as a web page.

2. Choose **File ➤ Export** from iPhoto's menu bar.

3. In the Export Photos window that appears, select the Web Page tab (Figure 10–24).

4. You'll see a host of settings to choose from. They are divided into three main sections: page, thumbnail, and image.

   ■ **Page:** Choose the title of your web page, how many columns and rows of photos you want displayed, the page template (plain or framed), and the background and text colors.

   ■ **Thumbnail:** Choose the maximum width and height of your photo thumbnails; then select whether to show the photo descriptions and titles on the web page.

   ■ **Image:** Choose the maximum width and height of a single photo when viewed on the web page, and then select whether to show the photo's description, title, metadata (EXIF), and location information on the web page.

5. After you have chosen your settings, click **Export**, and a Finder dialog box will appear.

6. Choose where you want to save the web page files, and then click the OK button. The web page files are exported, and you can then upload them to a server of your choice.

In Figure 10–25 you can see what a simple web page created by iPhoto looks like.

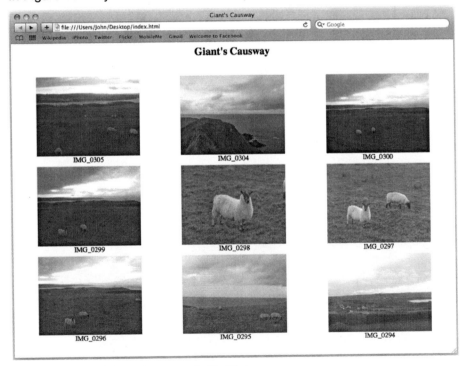

Figure 10–25. *A simple web page created in iPhoto*

QuickTime Movie

You can export a collection of your photos as a simple QuickTime movie (Figure 10–26). This movie can then be played on any Mac or PC using QuickTime Player or any other application or device that supports QuickTime movies.

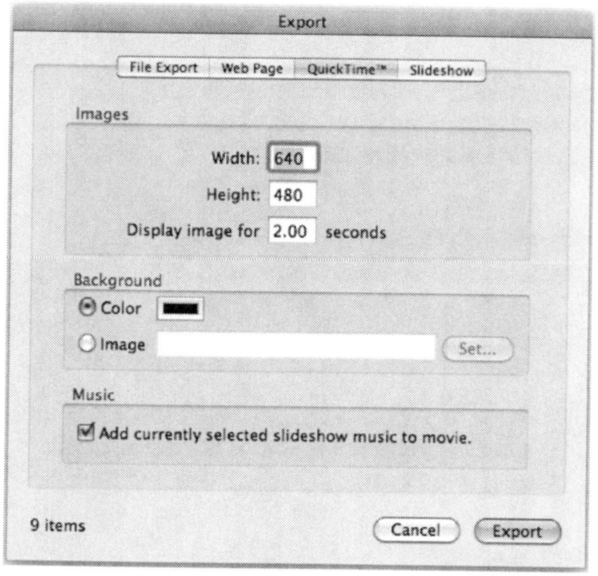

Figure 10–26. *Exporting your photos as a QuickTime movie*

To export photos as a QuickTime movie, follow these steps:

1. Select the photo or photos in your iPhoto Library that you want to export as a web page.

2. Choose File ➤ Export from iPhoto's menu bar.

3. In the Export Photos window that appears, select the QuickTime tab (Figure 10–26).

4. You'll see a variety of settings to choose from. They are divided into three man sections: images, background, and music.

    ▪ **Images:** Choose the width and height of the photos used in your movie, and then choose how long to display each photo for before moving on to the next one.

- **Background:** Choose the background color of your movie. If there is any space between the photos in your movie and the edge of the frame, that space will be filled with whatever background color you choose. Alternately, you can use an image from your computer as a background fill. To do so, select Image, click the Set button, and then choose the image file from the Finder window that appears and click Open.

- **Music:** Check this box if you want to apply iPhoto's last-used slideshow music as the background music for your QuickTime movie. If this box is unchecked, no music is exported with the movie.

5. After you have chosen your settings, click **Export**, and a Finder dialog box appears. Name your movie, choose where you want to save it, and then click the **OK** button.

Slideshow

The final Export tab allows you to quickly assemble a slideshow into a MPEG-4 file to use on multiple devices, including iPods, iPhone, iPads, Apple TVs, computers, and the Web (Figure 10–27).

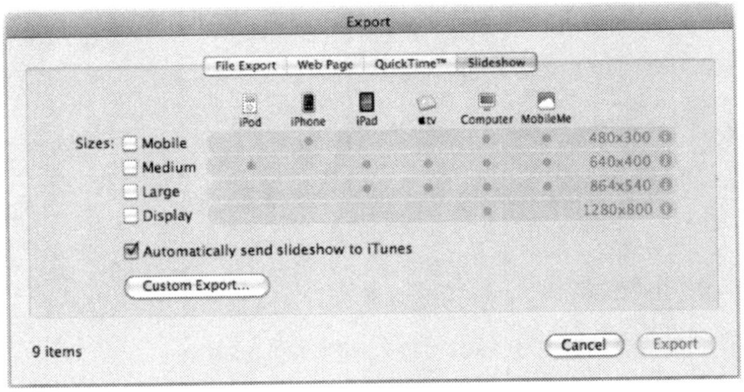

Figure 10–27. *Exporting your photos as slideshow MPEG-4 file*

To export photos as a slideshow MPEG-4 file, follow these steps:

1. Select the photo or photos in your iPhoto Library that you want to export as a slideshow.

2. Choose **File ➤ Export** from iPhoto's menu bar.

3. In the Export Photos window that appears, select the Slideshow tab (Figure 10–27).

4. Choose the size of the slideshow that best corresponds to the device you will be using it on.

5. If you are going to be using the slideshow on an iPod, iPhone, or iPad, check the **Automatically send slideshow to iTunes** box. This ensures that the slideshow is synced to your iOS device the next time you connect it to your Mac.

6. (Optional) You can specify a number of custom export options by clicking the **Custom Export** button. These options include device optimization and video, sound, and Internet streaming settings.

7. When you are ready to export your slideshow, click the **Export** button. A Finder dialog box appears. Choose where you want to save your slideshow, and then click the OK button.

Summary

From full-screen viewing to advanced export handling, iPhoto '11 offers you a wide range of settings to get the most out of your photos. As you can probably see from this chapter, you don't need to memorize these tools and settings to enjoy iPhoto; however, know that they are there and available to you should you need them. If you take only one thing away from this chapter, make sure that it is that backing up your iPhoto Library is an important and regular process you should be following. Our photos are our best lifeline to our memories. Make sure you protect them.

Index

■P

CPSIA information can be obtained at www.ICGtesting.com
228822LV00003B/13/P